How to Understand the Liturgy

Jean Lebon

How to Understand
the Liturgy

SCM PRESS LTD

Translated by Margaret Lydamore and John Bowden from the French
Pour vivre la liturgie
published 1986 by Les Editions du Cerf,
29 bd Latour-Maubourg, Paris

© Les Editions du Cerf 1986

Translation © Margaret Lydamore and John Bowden 1987

Nihil obstat: Father Anton Cowan
Censor

Imprimatur: Rt Rev. John Crowley, VG
Bishop in Central London
Westminster, 14 June 1987

The Nihil obstat *and* Imprimatur *are a declaration
that a book or pamphlet is considered to be free from
doctrinal or moral error. It is not implied that those who
have granted the* Nihil obstat *and* Imprimatur *agree
with the contents, opinions or statements expressed.*

British Library Cataloguing in Publication Data

Lebon, Jean
How to understand the liturgy.
1. Public worship
I. Title   II. Pour vivre la liturgie
English
264   BV10.2
ISBN 0–334–02039–5

First published in English 1987
by SCM Press Ltd, 26–30 Tottenham Road, London N1

Typeset at The Spartan Press Ltd, Lymington, Hants
and printed in Great Britain by Richard Clay plc, Bungay

Contents

References in italics are to the material in boxes

PART TWO

The Christian Liturgy

PART THREE

The Eucharistic Liturgy

By Way of Conclusion

Preface to the English Edition

An understanding of the liturgy does not come naturally. It is based on certain Christian truths that are basic to all Christian liturgy. These in turn suggest actions (rites) and attitudes that are fundamentally human. For if the content of the liturgy is divinely given, its many forms are man-made and in celebration involve the whole human personality both as an individual and as a member of the assembly that constitutes the liturgical community.

The great value of Fr Jean Lebon's book is that it lays out the underlying truths clearly and applies them to the celebration of the eucharistic liturgy. Noteworthy are his exposition of the nature of the assembly as the subject of celebration and his clear yet profound explanation of symbolism without which the liturgy cannot exist. Likewise, his treatment of the ministry of the word, something that is often handled perfunctorily in celebration, illuminates its high importance and significance. It is a dialogue with *God* in which the Holy Spirit is operative.

In the second half of the book the author ranges over the whole liturgy of the eucharistic action, commenting on each part from the presentation of the gifts to the dismissal. But all these parts are related to one another so that by the end of the book the reader is presented with a comprehensive whole.

Scattered up and down the book are practical suggestions to facilitate good celebration. The French often bring to their celebrations a quality of (informed) imagination that is all too little found, in Britain at any rate. We might do likewise.

Finally, Fr Lebon is both a liturgical scholar and a musician with a long experience in the promotion of good liturgical celebration. Readers will find here a sound introduction to the liturgy of the eucharist and much that is enlightening and practically helpful. For these reasons I am happy to recommend this book to clergy and laity in both Britain and the United States.

J. D. Crichton

The General Instruction of the Roman Missal is frequently quoted, particularly in Part Three, and is indicated by the abbreviation GIRM. The French term *animateur*, for which there is no exact equivalent in English, has usually been rendered either 'leader', 'commentator' or 'cantor'; for a fuller comment see the box on page 82.

Text which appears in this type is in the nature of an aside and addressed primarily to clergy.

PART ONE

Celebrating

1

When People Celebrate

'National holiday', 'An invitation to the wedding of X and Y', 'Tomorrow is Z's birthday'. None of these announcements of a celebration conjure up theories, or ideologies, or indeed any particular feelings in us to begin with. But pictures spring to mind at once: the wreath placed on the war memorial as the band plays its solemn music, the wedding reception and its centrepiece, the birthday presents and the cake with its candles. In other words, both the term celebration and what it denotes are associated with images and symbolic actions.

The same is true of the eucharist: there are the actions of the priest and the faithful, hymns, music and so on.

In order to understand the liturgy we must take a good look at what symbols are, since they are basic to all human experience and are the foundation stone of Christian liturgy, which to all intents and purposes is made up of symbolic actions.

The subject is a complex one, but I shall try to treat it simply and as far as possible avoid the jargon which specialists have to use, concentrating mainly on what is fairly self-evident as confirmation for some points which I think it important to make in order to further understanding of the liturgy and the Christian faith.

The signifier and the signified

Every human expression consists of something

1

that signifies and something that is signified. In France, I go into a baker's, point to a loaf and say 'Du pain, s'il vous plait'. The finger which I point and the sound 'pain' are what signifies, and the flour that has been leavened and baked is what is signified. In other words, to convey my meaning to this French baker I have used two codes: my pointing finger and a particular sound.

Sign and symbol

But sometimes things can happen differently.

To take another example: social convention (the Highway Code) dictates that when I see a red light I equate this with danger; I am firmly told 'No'. It is still a sign. The traffic authorities have passed a message on to me, and all they want is for me to take notice of it.

But when I see the colour red on my national flag or on a cardinal's robe or on a priest's red chasuble, something else happens. The colour red (that which signifies) reminds me, or can remind me, not only of what is signified but also of other things: blood, revolution, fire, love, the Holy Spirit, and so on. It is a symbol.

When people celebrate they certainly use signs ('Three cheers' or 'Let us pray', depending on whether the occasion is a celebratory speech or a religious service), but more than anything else they use symbols. The wreath at the Cenotaph also has other associations – death, life, remembrance, recognition and so on. The wedding reception stands for love, happiness, ongoing life. The cake with candles which have to be blown out stands for life (breath), growth, the past, affection and so on.

A house with two storeys

In practice, although the distinction is important, it is not always clear-cut. The colour red was chosen for its particular purpose in the Highway Code because it is the most visible, but also because of its subconscious association with blood.

But the opposite is even more true: a symbol is first of all a sign. It conveys a message to me. If I see a clergyman dressed in scarlet I immediately say to myself, 'There's a cardinal!' But the scarlet also acts on me as a symbol. In May 1968, as a school teacher, I watched the arrival of my young pupils, excitedly shouting out, 'Sir, there's a red flag on the factory next door.' The message had got home to them (the factory was on strike), but their excitement proved that the colour red had acted on them as a symbol.

You might see it in terms of a house the ground floor of which is the sign and the floor above the symbol. Or, to take another simple example: if I am in a foreign country and someone invites me to a meal but I don't understand the invitation (the sign), I cannot grasp the fact that this person is being friendly towards me (the symbol). We shall be noting the same point in connection with the eucharistic bread which must first of all be bread (a sign) if it is to be the symbol of quite another reality (see page 137).

Symbols are gratuitous

Unlike signs, symbols serve no useful purpose. We do not eat birthday cake for its nutritional value, nor do we put candles on it for the light that they shed; nor do we put flowers on the war memorial in order to make it look pretty. We do not go to the holy table, the altar, to feed ourselves. A symbol is not useful; painters and poets are not useful; the liturgy is not useful, at least in the utilitarian sense as understood by our technological and consumer societies. Symbols are gratuituous.

In inverted commas

In order to make an object, a gesture or a word into a symbol, I have to take it out of its normal context. Bakeries are full of bread, nurseries are full of flowers and shrubs.

But when a lover offers a rose to the girl of his dreams, or a head of state is presented with a bunch of roses, the flowers become a symbol of something quite different. Men and women gather together Sunday by Sunday to offer up and feed on a piece of bread; and the bread becomes a symbol, a sacrament of Someone.

Using something as a symbol means putting it between quotation marks. It means using a sign (a candle, for instance) out of its normal everyday context (a candle is usually lit to provide light) in such a way as to cause a shock. Taken to extremes, even the most mundane objects (such as a hammer and sickle!) can become symbols; even the least gifted person can become a living symbol of the unity of a kingdom.

Symbols create meaning

When my cat meows at the door, it is because he wants to come in; when my dog wags his tail, it is because he is pleased. The most developed animals also use signs, but never symbols.

The meaning of a sign is clearly defined, precise. In English, the word rose denotes a particular kind of flower, and (depending on the language) the words 'bread' or 'pain' or 'Brot' stand for the food with which we are all familiar.

In the case of a symbol the meaning is always new and unlimited. As long as there have been roses they have been a means of expressing love, life (but with undertones of sufferings, since 'there is no rose without a thorn') and youth ('Gather ye rosebuds while ye may'). Although bread has been somewhat devalued in our present-day society (in my childhood it was thought to be a 'crime' to throw bread away) it does symbolize our daily food, our daily work (earning one's bread), friendship (breaking bread together), the trials of everyday living, etc.

As always when talking about symbols, as you will already have noticed, one has to add etcetera, because one can never exhaust the meaning of a symbol.

Signs are always well-defined, labelled, distinctive. Everything has a place in the little pigeon-holes of the mind. Everything has a clear and straightforward meaning; a cat is a cat.

But with symbols everything is left open. Since the creation, humanity has kept discovering new meanings in the presents we give or the bread we share.

It is true that where symbols are concerned there are always blurred edges (and people who like everything to be well defined don't like blurred edges), a degree of ambivalence: the good bread which one is proud to share can turn stale; the wine drunk at the feast has bitter dregs; a rose has thorns, and the liturgical symbols of water and fire, which are sources of life, are also forces of destruction.

You can never get to grips with a symbol; if you try, you destroy it. Unlike a sign, which belongs to the sphere of knowledge, a symbol is a means of arriving at new insights. We shall see how this happens in the next chapter.

When we can find no words . . .

At times of crisis (when we are deeply moved, inexpressibly happy, terribly sad) we fall back on symbols; when there are 'no words to express what we want to say', when joy or grief or sympathy go beyond words, when the contemplation of a great mystery takes our breath away – what other means of communication is open to us? Silence, certainly – but isn't this itself symbolic? More than anything else, there is the symbolic gesture. Read the parable of the Prodigal Son in Luke 15 once again. Notice the father: what does he do to express his unspeakable joy (which is at the heart of the parable)? 'He ran to meet him, flung his arms around his neck and kissed him.' Then he gave orders for the feast. The cloak, the ring, the shoes were brought out – but above all, 'Bring out the fatted calf, kill it, let us eat and rejoice.' And there was music and dancing. Not a great many words here, except for the joyful refrain, 'My son was dead and is alive again.'

Symbolism is the point at which language overflows. So we can understand why Christian celebration, which claims to reveal the Wholly Other, the Ineffable, the Inexpressible, the invisible God, more than any other human celebration expresses itself in symbols.

Sacrament

The word sacrament (*sacramentum*) has several equivalents in theological language. First of all there is the word mystery (Greek *mysterion*), not in the sense of something more or less incomprehensible but in its biblical sense of a 'divine plan' which is manifested and put into effect in Jesus Christ (for example in St Paul's Letter to the Romans, 16.25f.). What was visible in Christ is now visible in the sacraments.

The word sacrament is also quite often defined as a sign which produces the grace which it signifies. It would be better to talk of it in terms of a symbol, or even more precisely of a symbolic sign.

The liturgy is at the same time both a sign and a symbol. It is a sign, in the sense that it relates to the ultimate one who is signified, namely God. When 'the fashion of this world passes away' we shall no longer need signifiers: we shall see 'God as he is', as the liturgy puts it (I John 3.2).

But it is also a symbol. All that we do in it relates to Christ, who signifies God, 'the image of the invisible God' (St Paul).

The 'mixture of symbols'

If we juxtapose a number of symbols in time and space the link produces new significances.

A simple example is the difference between putting a bunch of flowers on a tomb, on the altar, or in the hall. The shaded areas are the significances that I leave to experience:

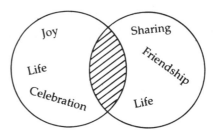

Bunch of flowers   Altar

There are plenty of liturgical examples of this 'mixing'.

2

They Recognize One Another

A story of tokens

Underlying the word symbol, which comes from the Greek, is the idea of being 'thrown together'. Amongst the Greeks a *symbolon* was a kind of token, an object cut in two, of which each party to the contract took one piece. It is said that this practice still goes on today among some secret societies, who use a bank note. Neither piece has any value of its own, but when they are put together they are a sign of recognition.

'They knew him in the breaking of the bread'

A symbol is a kind of password, an exchange between people.

A symbol establishes a relationship. When I go to the baker to buy bread, I have virtually no relationship with him, and even if I do, it is quite irrelevant to my purchase. I am on the level of the sign, and the only thing that matters is the message.

But when I break bread (or share a meal) with friends, I am entering into a relationship with them. In the case of the symbol, the relationship is more important than what is communicated. A sign belongs in the order of knowledge; a symbol in the order of recognition. By means of symbols people can recognize themselves (rediscover themselves) and one another (what binds them together). 'They knew him in the breaking of the bread' says St Luke of the disciples on the road to

Emmaus . . . And undoubtedly it was this gesture too that enabled them to recognize themselves as disciples of the crucified and risen Lord, since they then became bearers of the good news by returning to Jerusalem and the trials that awaited them.

A means of identification

A symbol always has a social dimension.

A national flag, or hymn, or holiday allows a nation to recognize itself as a social, political and geographical entity. Every political, cultural and educational movement, every group of human beings, gives itself an identity by means of symbolic actions, which allow an individual to integrate himself or herself with a group and a group to make itself distinctive, to place itself in relation to the rest of society.

In the same way a Christian identifies himself or herself as a member of the church by taking the body of Christ in communion or by reciting the Apostles' or Niceno-Constantinopolitan creed (which in the original Latin and Greek was in fact called a symbol). By meeting together regularly (the assembly is itself a symbol, see page 32) the group defines itself and presents a front to the rest of the world.

This is also the way in which non-Christians recognize Christians: they know that they 'go to Mass'. Of course the symbol does not mean to them what it means to us, because they are not part of the family. And I am not forgetting Jesus' saying 'Love one another . . . by this people shall know that you are my disciples.' We shall come to see how the symbol must go hand in hand with everyday life, but to love one's brothers and sisters is it enough to recognize one another (do not the 'heathen' love one another too?) if the commandment to love is not also recognized through a symbol? This symbol, in other words the liturgy, is absolutely necessary both for others, so that they can recognize us, and for

ourselves, Christians scattered through the world, so that we can recognize one another 'as his disciples'.

Different but united

When we hear our national anthem, we feel a sense of national identity. A national symbol does not remove internal disagreements, but it allows them to be transcended. Undoubtedly it is this national feeling, continually nourished and renewed by national festivals, which allows all the different elements in a country to put on a united front when a serious danger threatens it. This was well demonstrated, for example, in the French Resistance, when men and women of all persuasions fought side by side against Nazi Germany, 'those of all beliefs and of none'.

Whereas a sign focusses a thin beam of light on a particular point, a symbol scans a wide arc. We know very well that the same celebration is experienced by those who take part in it in the same way, and yet at the same time differently. The experience of a golden wedding is quite different for the couple themselves from the experience of that golden wedding by their children, their grandchildren or a relative who has just lost her husband. It is the same when a liturgical team looks back on a celebration, and its members find to their surprise that even those who planned it have experienced it in different ways.

This is also the case when a symbol is on the level of a relationship between people who are all different and who live different lives. Moreover, the same person can discover different meanings in the same celebration on different occasions; when I take communion, on one Sunday I experience it as communion with the suffering Christ, on another Sunday as communion with the risen Christ and on yet another Sunday as communion with my brothers and sisters. Of course, all these meanings are always present, but at different times something in me makes me more sensitive to one or the other.

A symbol is neither subjective nor objective.

It is not subjective, in the sense that anyone can see what he or she likes in it, because there is always a core of meaning on which all are agreed. Nor is it objective, because what is signified is never automatic. A symbol is relationship, experience.

There is another way of checking on a liturgy. When you hear young people going out of a Mass saying, 'That was great' and old people saying 'that was a good mass', something has certainly worked on the symbolic side. And having noticed it many times, I am persuaded that even young children have a sense of liturgy in a parish community provided that the symbolism is good. If that does not happen, and they get bored, there may be two causes: either they have not been taught enough about Christianity (and that, unfortunately, is most often the case), or the liturgy has been reduced to talking (and that, sadly, is also frequent), since children are naturally open to symbolic language, like poets and artists.

The whole person

A symbol unites people, and it also makes a person whole. In contrast to a sign, which is primarily concerned with our ablty to learn, a symbol takes over the whole person – our intelligence, certainly, but also our senses, our emotions, our imagination – in short, our whole body.

We shall be coming back to the importance of the body in the liturgy, but at this stage let us just note that in symbolic action, and therefore in the liturgy, first of all there are things to see, hear, touch, taste and feel; there are body movements, gestures. This is what our childhood catechism meant when it spoke of outward signs. A symbol takes us over completely.

A chance offered

Because it is to do with the whole person, because it is a link, a recognition, a pact, an alliance between human beings (and, where the liturgy is concerned, between human beings and God), a symbol is an experience of relationship.

In a relationship, everyone is free, free to come and go, free to welcome meaning. Everyone can retain his or her own identity, and live in a true relationship.

A symbol is a proposition. Unlike a sign, one can never fully grasp the effects of a symbol. One can plan symbols, but one can never anticipate what is going to happen to those who take part in them. It is more likely to be the symbol which grasps us. A symbol is an opportunity which is always being offered to us. We should trust it.

3

The Experience of Symbols

Gaining access to reality, all reality: Embodying reality

The world needs artists and poets. Unfortunately it is all too easy for us to guess what a society would be like which believed only in science and technology. Pure intelligence gives us access only to part of reality. The poet, the artist, the mystic, take other ways and can claim to grasp a reality which is much broader, much higher or much deeper, which cannot be quantified and which is difficult to define. They are explorers of meaning. And that is why they often go mad . . .

The author of Genesis was a poet in his own way. The organization of the universe as he describes it, following the manner of the cosmogonies of his time, has long since become outdated. (Voltaire already mocked it.) But the meaning of this creation is always true, and we shall never finish discovering it.

The poet, the artist, the liturgy do not seek first to give us a message, but lead us to an experience. They say to us: 'Through my poem, my picture, my rites, allow yourself to penetrate a universe which your eyes cannot see and your intelligence alone cannot apprehend.' And the most knowledgeable theologian must undergo a symbolic experience to have personal experience of this God whom he has constantly scrutinized through his intelligence: 'I thank you, Father, that you have hidden this from the wise and knowing, but have revealed it to the little ones.' Do we not have to have the soul of a child to be able to accept symbolic experience? 'When we get excited over some celebration, don't people say to us, 'You big babies!' A capacity for wonder, for getting out of one's aloofness, daring to make gestures which, seen from outside the experience, might seem puerile or crazy. The symbol is a door opening on reality, on condition that one is moved by it, allows oneself to act through it.

The liturgy: words and actions

When a child offers its mother a present or flowers on Mothering Sunday, the gesture expresses love and gratitude.

As I said earlier, there is an element of message, sign, information in a symbol. But it is not the essential part. When a lover says to his girl friend 'I love you', he is not imparting information (she does not reply, 'Yes, I know, you've told me that a thousand times.' He would be disturbed if she did). This is an example of a symbolic phrase (which is more action than word, as we shall see in the next chapter); as he says that, his love grows and takes shape. This word expresses, but above all 'makes', love.

When I receive the consecrated bread the person giving it to me says 'the body of Christ'. This is a very good elliptical phrase because I can understand it to mean either, 'Yes, indeed, this bread is the body of Christ', or, 'We are the body of Christ'. Above all, however, by receiving the Body of Christ I become a little more a member of this body. The symbol (the sacrament) produces in me what it signifies. In this action and this word (symbolic signs) there is a theology (the order of the sign) and above all there is what one might call a theurgy (-urgy as in metallurgy), in other words an operation, a transformation.

So the symbol brings me into contact with a Reality, essentially by acting on me, in me.

Finally, the symbol makes the reality present. At the level of signs I can pronounce words to go with a present or a bunch of flowers, words of love and thanks, without doing anything to make these realities real.

By contrast, on the symbolic level the fact of offering a present or a bunch of flowers (assuming, of course, that this is really a present), brings into existence the realities of love and gratitude. The fact of receiving the consecrated bread brings into existence the reality of communion with Christ. The fact of being baptized makes me a member of Christ.

Now this is not a comparison, in terms of 'I am united to Christ as the bread is united to my body', or united to my friends 'as the grains of flour are in the host', or 'I am immersed in water as Christ was immersed in death'. Certainly this aspect of comparison exists, but it is stronger than that.

The reality signified is not 'alongside' (*parabole*) but joined to (*sym-bole*) what it signifies. In a mere message the sign tends to efface itself once the message has been given. By contrast, symbol and reality coexist. The symbol has to remain for the reality to be signified.

To go back to the example of baptism: I am not immersed in water as Christ was immersed in death, but by being immersed in water I am immersed in the death of Christ, to emerge from it alive. 'The truth of baptism, as of all sacraments, is to be found only at the heart of the symbolic action and in accordance with it' (L.-M. Chauvet). Certainly we try to live out the reality of our baptism all through our life by 'getting wet' for the cross, not hesitating to be immersed with it in the combat of Life against Death. That does not prevent this immersion in the act of baptism being very real.

A reality hidden and revealed

Our God is on the one hand a hidden God, a God

Offertory table. Engraving. Jean Bertholle. *Photo F. Boissonnet*

10

we cannot grasp, a silent God, the great Absence, and on the other hand God revealed, made manifest, God the Word, the great Presence. We also find this paradoxical truth in the mystery of Jesus. On the one hand he reveals the Father ('He who has seen me has seen the Father') and on the other hand he hides God, he is a stone of stumbling, a scandal for believing Jews. To discover God in him we have to have confidence in him, put our trust in him, be acted on by him.

The same goes for liturgical and sacramental action. It hides from us the mystery of God and at the same time reveals it to us. We have to allow ourselves to be acted on by it, or rather by the Christ who, in the Church's faith, acts by it.

A plea for the body

If need be, one can do without any objects in celebration; but one can never do without the body. The whole of the Western world has relegated the body to second place and glorified the intelligence, cerebrality (hence, as a reaction, the success of all the Eastern techniques). There are those who attribute this mistrust of the body to a Jewish-Christian tradition: they have never read the Bible or the Psalms, in which the body is always present. Human beings have been saved in their entirety, body and soul. 'That which was from the beginning, which we have heard, which we have seen with our eyes, which we have looked upon and touched with our hands, concerning the word of life . . . we proclaim also to you' (I John 1.1–3).

Now our body is of prime concern in symbolic action because it is a place of relationship, relationship with creation (above all space), with others, with God. We have only to see how our attitudes, our gestures, our looks and even the timbre of our voices change depending on the relationship that we have with that which is not ourselves.

If we want to enter into a relationship with God or help others to do so, we have to renew acquaintance with our body. We concern ourselves with music to sing, prayers to recite, texts to read, but we remain outside things without becoming physically involved in them. We forget that singing involves the whole body, that it is first of all a matter of praying, that it is first of all a matter of proclaiming a text by communicating it with one's breath and voice, and so on.

Actions speak. When friends are in distress, a handclasp or a gentle embrace bring us nearer to them than any word. Our actions speak louder than our words. And in the liturgy, too, what we do counts more than anything we say. We waste our breath preaching that the church is not just the hierarchy if in fact everything in our congregations is clericalized. We can trot out words like brotherly and sisterly community, communion, but if the congregation does not form such a community, for example by sitting together instead of being spread all over the nave, and if no one takes any notice of his or her neighbour, whatever we say is useless. That is why the church has always seen in its liturgy what specialists call a 'theological locus', that is to say a place which teaches us something of the Christian faith.

4

Liturgy is Action

As I have said, the symbol acts in us; it is operational, it does things, but at the same time we have to perform it, to set it to work. I think that this point needs to be stressed in a world in which there is more speaking and writing than ever before, in which day by day we are flooded with a mass of information. The Church of our day does not escape this perpetual commentary. But the liturgy is primarily action. And as you will have noted, while I have often talked about a symbol, I should have always talked about a symbolic action. An object is never symbolic in itself: it becomes symbolic when it is the back-up to an action, a gesture. Flowers, a light, water, a flag are not symbolic in themselves: what are symbolic are the flowers that I offer, the light that

I kindle or pass on, the water that I pour on someone or in which I am immersed, the flag that I wave. At least objects always relate to an action: thus the flag that I see on the front of a building has been put there by someone with a specific intention, and the full sense of the reservation of the eucharistic host which I adore can only be grasped in connection with the action of the eucharist.

Furthermore, many symbolic actions, like gestures, songs and words, do not involve a material object.

Letting the symbol speak

Certainly celebration cannot do without words.

But first it is necessary to present the symbol correctly, to allow it to express all its potentialities so that these can be potentialities for us.

As I have already stressed, the symbol speaks to all our being, but particularly to our body and all its senses. So it is essential that what holds our attention, what we can see, touch, smell, or taste, speaks for itself; it is essential that the actions that we perform or the way in which we hold our bodies in space speak for themselves.

Let the symbol speak for itself, at the very heart of the symbolic action, before we try to talk about it! That is how our forefathers in the faith, in the first centuries of the Church, understood things.

In these ancient times it was around the sacrament that all symbolism was developed (you can find examples in the New Testament itself, in I Peter 2.1–10 or Romans 6–8) and its consequences for Christian life. This is what has been called 'mystagogy'. Provided that the person concerned has heard the gospel beforehand, he or she is not really initiated into the sacrament; the sacrament itself is the initiation. First one acts, then one speaks. The quality of symbolic action is a vitally important matter for the reality that we celebrate and therefore for faith.

The disputes which followed the reforms of Vatican II related more to questions of form than verbal content: Gregorian chant, Masses with guitar accompaniment, the host placed in the hand. Here is proof that what the Church actually does has greater impact than what it says.

But saying is also doing. When a mayor gives a speech on a great civic occasion he may well have something particular to say to his fellow citizens. But at the same time his appearance as first citizen of his city is also symbolic. How many official speeches are uninteresting in content – yet it would be wrong if they were not made at all.

In our service we also need speeches, a variety of comments in which a message is being delivered; at the same time, however, most of what is said has a symbolic character. In giving his greeting the priest faces the congregation, and this greeting symbolizes, makes, the structure of the Church. When a lay person says something, by way of testimony or in giving notices (see page 142), he or she symbolizes very markedly (above all today in contrast with the past) the responsibility of the people of God, independently of what he or she actually says.

We need to go further and speak of 'sacramental words' (the absolution, or the words of consecration, or those that go with the pouring of water at baptism). These are sometimes seen as magic words, above all the consecration: the use of the word 'formula' in connection with them is very revealing. We shall be coming back in chapter 14 to the specific nature of the sacrament and the link between word and action, but it is important to observe that the 'efficacy' of these words is rooted in their nature as symbolic words. I have already pointed out the performative (for what this word means see page 60) character of the 'I love you' said by the lover. It's the same with sacramental words: to say 'This is my body' is to say 'I forgive you'; it is to bring into effect God's pardon.

Not an explanation

A symbol does not give an explanation. It does not speak of itself, but itself speaks to us. We are taught to say hello ('Say hello to . . .'), to give presents, before we are given any kind of explanation. If there ever was one.

Imagine someone saying, 'I'm shaking your hand because it means . . .' or 'I'm kissing you because a kiss means . . . ' There may indeed be a historical explanation of a handshake (proof that the right hand, the one which usually carried a weapon, was innocent of any aggressive intent?) or a psychological explanation of a kiss ('I would so like to eat you . . .', 'you taste good'), but these 'explanations' only interest specialists.

A symbol does not give an explanation. If we had learned that, our celebrations would not be so full of innumerable commentaries: 'Now the priest is going to do this because . . .', 'Now we shall sing such and such because . . .'

If we had understood that, we would not take the wrong course of initiating children into the Mass, changing the Mass itself into a catechesis. Of course the celebration has to be adapted to the cultural and psychological possibilities of this age, but first of all it is necessary to help young people to become involved. Then, if need be, words will be added not so much to explain as to help them bring out the meaning of what they have done, to make it specific, to give it a place in the totality of their awakening to faith, in other words to link this experience to other experiences.

A symbol does not give an explanation. In the examples which I have given on these pages I have had to work out its function, but we can only do that by appealing to experiences which have already taken place, without being able to prejudge experiences to come. In the end, at the risk of sawing off the branch on which I am sitting, would not this book be unnecessary if symbols were always put to work perfectly? But . . . , but . . .

Signs which signify

For the symbol to work, what it signifies has to be significant. Here is an anecdote. As a very young priest I was taken to celebrate a baptism in a parish with which I was not familiar. After the baptism, the parish priest, who had been there, said to me: 'Father, I noticed that you poured the water on the child's skull; don't you know that if there is a lot of hair so as to prevent the water touching the actual skin, the baptism is not valid?' I did not know what to reply, with the objects used in baptism still vivid in my mind: the jug of stagnant water at the bottom of the font, the rather doubtful cloth and the salt (they were still using it) in a salt-cellar with holes in, which irresistibly made me think of the ones I used to apply vigorously to my portions of French fries.

The signs did not speak or delivered the wrong message. How did the symbols of life, welcome, belonging to Christ (Christ = the anointed one) function? God only knows. I also think of this priest during funerals, saying splendid things about the baptism of the dead person, when the whole congregation knew perfectly well that there was no holy water in the vessel and after the so-called aspersion one heard the metallic sound of the banging of the sprinkler on the bottom of the holy water vat.

Not to mention thuribles which have gone out, electric candles and other fakes! We shall often be talking about the truth of signs.

5

The Rite

Having explored the riches of symbolic action, we now come to the idea of the rite, with which it is closely linked.

Ritual is a word that we use in a matter of fact way: 'Whenever he went down to the market he had a ritual of dropping into the bar for a drink.' Even this weak sense of the word ritual tells us that the notion behind it is one of custom, repetitiveness.

In the strong sense and in our present context we can define a rite as a symbolic action (or group of symbolic actions) which are repeated regularly and which have prescribed forms (tacitly or explicitly).

Human beings are ritual animals

Rites are not restricted to the liturgy. In fact, from earliest childhood on we are as it were programmed to say hello, to kiss or shake hands, to behave at table, and so on. Wherever people are together, rites tend to develop.

The claim that rites are unnecessary, which has sometimes been made in the name of progress, renewal, or sincerity, is a denial of a basic element of human nature. Men and women are ritual animals: a couple will have their own little rites for celebrating their love; a group of veterans will meet regularly at the same place and follow a well established ritual; political movements have their ritual celebrations on national festivals, and so on. I have shown how symbolic action allows individuals or groups to recognize one another at the deepest level of their identity. So it is logical that when one finds a good symbolic expression, one wants to repeat it. And when the reality celebrated does not change and the group recognizes itself in it, why should one change the forms – the rites – of celebration? For as we have already seen, the meaning is attached to the form.

Rites are social practices. When I want to join a group, I may hear the voice of the group telling me, 'That's how we do things. These are our customs and everyone likes them, they all recognize themselves in them. Come and do as we do. You're free, but if you want to be one of us, you must observe our rites.'

So if I want to enter this community (I the neophyte, the catechumen, the postulant, the novice, the fresher), I agree to undergo a ritual, the ritual that the older members of the group have already undergone. In a word, I am initiated (from the Latin *initium* = beginning, go in).

Initiation, in other words integration into the group by means of a symbolic practice, is only possible if it is ritualized.

A source of freedom

Because the word 'habits' often has pejorative connotations – routine, well-worn, in a rut – and because at first sight rites and ritual suggest constraint, many people mistrust them.

However, one does not have to reflect for long to see that ritual habits are indispensable. It's a good thing that the hostess does not have to wonder every time whether the soup should come before or after the beef, the fish before or after the ice cream. Without knowing it, she is observing an established ritual, and that is all the better for her, since it leaves her free to bring this ritual alive as it stands by choosing a menu

in which the courses go well together. Again, it's a good thing that we do not have to think every time we greet someone: the established rite of saying 'Hello' or shaking hands which I can always perform allows me to put more or less into it, from a distant 'Hello' to a warm hand-shake and a big smile. It's a good thing that we don't have to reinvent the Mass every Sunday. That would be exhausting and unbearable.

Only within a ritual can our freedom move. Ritual is also a restraint on subjectivity, disorder and anarchy. Without it the celebration would soon be killed off by the 'inventions' of cranks, or delivered into the hands of those who want to make an impression. The ritual does not get in the way of feeling and emotion, but channels them, preventing the celebration from sinking into sentimentalism, emotionalism, romanticism. Spontaneity is a sheer illusion. More than

Photo C . I . M.

one informal group has felt this and has gradually imposed a ritual pattern on itself.

Time needed to take it in

Of course a symbolic action does not always make its mark immediately. Time is needed for taking it in. When looking at a picture or reading a poem we need time to get into it; we need to look at it a while, read and re-read it: it can stand up to that. So too with the liturgy: we do not get into a gesture, a chant, a process straight away. The repetition of the rite allows us to make these things truly ours, that much more each time we do them. And as the riches of the symbol are inexhaustible, one constantly finds new meanings in it (and we shall live with the eucharist till we die).

'The tradition received from the Lord'

The notion of a rite is also very much bound up with the idea of tradition. Tradition means transmission. Most of our social rites are inherited from the past, many of them lost in the mists of time (the Christmas tree, the mistletoe, midsummer fires, and so on) and they still 'function'.

Some people bristle at the idea of tradition, as if the long past of a rite was a defect. They are right, if maintaining a tradition is synonymous with sclerosis and conservatism, in which the rite is no longer at the service of humanity. With the liturgy, I would want to distinguish between the Tradition and the traditions. Let me explain. Every social group evolves; its culture evolves, and so, therefore, does its way of living and celebrating.

Social historians make a distinction which goes rather like this: first there is a secret group of rites and institutions (at this point the group is said to be in the 'instituting' stage). Then, gradually, these institutions are stabilized (and are said to have been 'instituted'). But as the group evolves, it challenges what has been 'instituted' and again starts 'instituting'. And so on. That is how the history of our rites goes. The social body of the Church certainly does not escape this evolutionary phenomenon. Look at the history of the great religious orders . . . In the liturgy, too, we cannot challenge what Paul calls 'the tradition received from the Lord' (I Cor. 11.23) in connection with the eucharist. Neither the broad outline of the Mass, nor the great symbols of the eucharist or of baptism can be changed, since these are fundamental signs of our Christian identity. But within the liturgy there are a great many secondary rites and practices which are more bound to a given culture (and which we adorn with the name of

---

Ritualism

The best of things can be perverted. So the rite can degenerate into ritualism. What do I mean by that?

I mean performing the rite for the rite's sake, forgetting why it is done and above all those for whom it is done. 'The sabbath was made for man, not man for the sabbath,' said Jesus. Instead of being the source of freedom, the rite becomes slavery. It can go hand in hand with legalism and a good conscience: 'I've done everything that had to be done as it ought to have been done', or even worse with Pharisaism: 'Woe to you, Pharisees, who purify the outside of the cup and the plate (rite) while inside it is full of extortion and rapacity (the significance of the rites)' (Matt. 23.25). Ritualism can even go as far as being idolatry, if to perform the rite is a way of laying hands on God.

Rubricism

Even where it does not get as far as being perverted, the performance of rites suffers more generally from an evil which, while forgivable in itself, is catastrophic for the life of the liturgy. I have called it 'rubricism', in other words scrupulous but superficial observation of the rubrics: those little notes in liturgical books, often printed in red, which indicate what is to be done and how to do it.

Rubricism consists in carrying out the instructions to the letter, but without putting even one's self into it, let alone one's faith or one's piety. Suppose I am told to hold out my arms: I hold them out, but the gesture is not really mine, and it loses all significance. Alternatively, the rite is performed without any concern for its purpose (for example, saying 'Let us pray' and then not leaving enough time for prayer) or for the congregation for whom it is intended.

A rubricist mentality is still widespread today. That can be explained in historical terms by the tension in the church in the face of the upsurge of the Reformation in the sixteenth century. Most priests were trained in this system, as indeed were laity, since the latter, too, are not free from rubricism. It is not uncommon after Mass to hear the reproach over a tiny change of detail: 'It's not in my missal!'

There are two ways of combatting this mentality: to get right to the heart of the rite and to know what the church seeks to do by offering it to us. If we achieve this, the rites, the actions, the words, the objects will of themselves find the most expressive way of being performed.

traditions).

That is why the liturgy must constantly be readjusted. And it has been with this readjustment, this *aggiornamento*, that Vatican II has been concerned. *Aggiornamento* is always necessary and it is no doubt because it has been awaited for so long that many people have found it so painful. That having been said, the Church cannot touch the tradition, nor does it want to; it can modify this or that peripheral rite, this or that detail in the sequence of rites, but it cannot for example alter the basic course of the eucharist without betraying the intention of its founder. The Church, and each of us who perform the liturgy, must constantly return to the sources of the New Testament and the first generations of Christians, still close in time to the Lord, not in order to reproduce to the last detail what was once done (that would be archaeology, since we live in a different culture), but so as always to have the intention of the Lord in mind.

Always the same, always new

Most parents will have heard their children complain, 'Oh, Mass, it's always the same.' Yes, it is always the same, just as saying hello, birthdays, parties are always the same. But it is always new. It is always new because those involved are different or have developed, because the history in which these actions are set has moved on.

The Mass is also always new (unless the rite has become fixed in a ritualistic way) because imagination has been shown within a liturgical pattern which is still respected: just as on birthdays the menu for the meal may alter and different people may be invited, and the presents will obviously be different. Effort will be made to 'find something new' while respecting the ritual programme. Why?

Rites get worn out

The previous pages have shown us good reasons for having rites. But rites are not only open to the deviations of ritualism and rubricism, but are also threatened with getting worn out. How many routine greetings there are, for example, in everyday life! In the liturgy, how many actions become automatic: making the sign of the cross (see pages 94.f), the actions of getting up or sitting down! It is by no means rare for the congregation to sit down immediately after the Amen at the absolution, confusing it with the Amen of the opening prayer. There are plenty of other examples: nor should we be shocked; it's human nature. But something must always be done to reduce this wearing away. How? Breaking up the rite? Certainly not.

The most important thing is to live out the rite from within.

Reviving meaning

The next thing is to change ritual habits very slightly so as to make a contrast with ordinary practice. A contrast attracts attention again and revives meaning. It attracts attention again: for example, while you've been reading these pages your attention will have been caught by a box or an illustration, and if you had been going off to sleep (which I hope was not the case), that will have made you alert again.

Contrast attracts attention again: you will find many suggestions as to how this may be done while reading the pages on the eucharist, but here is one. We get used to rites of consecration, and in particular bowing tends to become automatic: on Sundays when there is a particular celebration of the presence of the Lord the Body and Blood of Christ are censed and/or the people are invited to make a deep bow. The rite has not been suppressed, but the way of doing it has been slightly changed so that there is a chance of a contrast with other Sundays when the rite is performed in the usual way.

In other words, the rite is a canvas on which one can and must embroider, a bit like those stories of which the Bible offers several versions, or the kerygmatic scheme which also appears in several versions (see *How to Read the New Testament*, page 34).

But one has to know the canvas well . . .

6

Vatican II, A Revolution

Now that we have seen what celebration is, and before coming to Christian celebration, it will be useful to look at the liturgical reform introduced by Vatican II. Everyone knows the vast amount of work it involved and also the controversies and the opposition which it prompted.

The liturgy has been pruned, simplified, and stripped of rites which had become incomprehensible because they derived from another culture which was much more portentous than ours (for example in the canon the priest used to make the sign of the cross something like twenty-eight times). Once the purging of the rite had been completed, it had to be stressed by a return to the sources: a theology of the assembly, the importance of the liturgy of the word, the

restoration of basic rites like the prayer of the faithful and so on. In addition to all that came the extremely significant step of restoring the vernacular (see chapter 15).

A revolution in mentality

All that was the immediate and tangible aspect of the reform. And the great majority of Catholics were delighted by it. It has caused a good deal of ink to flow. However, that does not seem to me to have been the most revolutionary change. It has not been noticed that the change went much deeper than a modification of rites.

Before Vatican II, the ideal of the liturgist was to perform the 'ceremonies' detailed in the official books as scrupulously as possible. These official books were no more than an extremely detailed description of what had to be done.

One has only to open the liturgical books ('the rituals') of Vatican II – above all the most recent ones like that on penance – to see the change. Two essential modifications stand out:

1. Not content with saying what must be done, the books say why it is done (what I shall call the aim or even the function of the rite);

2. Many rites leave those who perform them some freedom of choice; very often, freedom to decide is left to each conference of bishops.

It follows from this that first, those (the person) responsible for the liturgy can no longer go to the sacristy at the last minute and embark on the liturgy head bowed (however piously) as though pedalling off on a bicycle. According to Vatican II the celebration presupposes pastoral choices and therefore requires preparation.

And secondly, knowledge of the liturgy can no longer be external and 'material'. It is not enough to know the letter; it is necessary to know the spirit.

The significance of present-day liturgical research

To show the revolution in the conception of rites I have drawn a diagram of the development prompted by Vatican II.

Two comments: 1. In describing the first stage, i.e. the situation before the Council, I have not been passing judgment on either the faith or the intelligence of our predecessors; they were neither less believing nor less shrewd than we are. But they lived in another system.

2. I have described these stages as if they all took place everywhere at the same time. In fact some celebrating communities are still at the second stage, if not the first.

To illustrate these stages I have taken a rite, the Alleluia, as an example (diagram 1).

First stage: Before Vatican II the priest (or the cantor) saw Alleluia in his missal (and the verse with it). The rite was performed without questions being asked. If it was a High Mass, the Alleluia was sung. Otherwise it was recited. There was no preoccupation with its meaning.

Second stage: the possibility of celebrating in the vernacular and the desire to do so led to the creation of a repertoire and at the same time a reflection on the aim of the rite: in this case acclamation (its function). So that it was possible for that to be done there was a re-examination of the old repertoire. Obviously the word Alleluia was not translated, but the verse which went with it was. Hence the discovery that Alleluia, Christ is risen, needs a chant if it is to be an acclamation. But because people still had their noses glued to the old models, these were copied, to produce neo-Gregorian, neo-classical and so on. In some cases Gregorian chant was still used, if only for the Alleluia. That in itself was an enormous step forward, as the rite had a chance of being significant.

Third stage: it very soon became evident that a

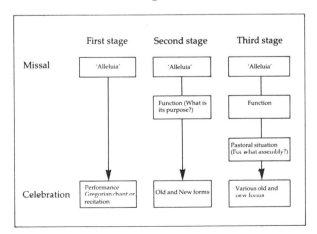

second dimension had to be introduced: the pastoral situation. Alleluia is an acclamation. In it, here the Church invites us to acclaim the word of God. But who is celebrating? What assembly? What are its culture, its feelings, its tastes? What are its resources in terms of singers and instruments? and so on.

In the light of these two factors, the ritual and the pastoral, the person in authority chooses the most suitable form. To give a few examples (somewhat schematically): one would not use the same musical form for a congregation of contemplatives (for which Gregorian chant might be suitable), a congregation of young people (rhythmical music), children (alleluia with clapping or arm movement), and a congregation which had a trained choir or a very gifted organist. (At a very similar rite, the acclamation which follows the exchange of vows at a marriage, when the congregation doesn't sing I ask the organist to play the acclamation, as a kind

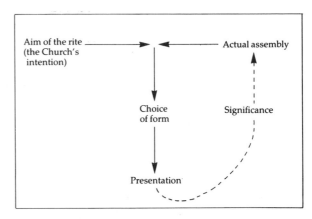

of brief musical fireworks.)

The diagram above sums up the course of liturgical work.

Why is the significance put as a dotted line? Because, as we have seen, we cannot control the effect of the symbol. We can only estimate it, not guarantee it. Liturgical work must be stamped with this humility!

A reform still to be achieved

Despite all the good intentions and the amount of time spent in the service of our congregations, it has to be recognized that this reform of attitudes towards the rite is far from universal. But we must not be pessimistic. Twenty years is not a long time in evolutionary terms, above all when the majority of those in charge of liturgy (priests, choirmasters, musicians, and so on) have been shaped (regimented?) by another

conception of the liturgy.

Moreover this change in mentality is all the more difficult to achieve when we are in a sphere where action is more decisive than thought: many people who gladly adopt the new perspective are held back by the weight of habit.

What is needed is time and patience; but the patience must be an active one.

PART TWO

The Christian Liturgy

7

When God Makes a Sign

The old covenant

We believe that it is possible for all men and women of good will to discover signs of God, whether by means of the wonders of creation or through meditation on the meaning of human existence. God is always making a sign to 'all who seek him with a sincere heart', as a eucharistic prayer puts it.

God always takes the initiative, even if religious people do not always recognize it. The Bible tells us that the initiative which God took was such an original one that, not content with revealing himself to humankind, God chose a people, Israel. In the first covenant God formed an association of which one might say that he was both the founder president and the partner.

It was already becoming apparent that the bond between humankind and God was truly parallel to that between human beings. Undoubtedly the discovery of a personal relationship with God continued to grow throughout the Old Testament, but the relationship was always lived out in the context of a communion of faith, love and hope.

God chose a people for himself (in Abraham), saved them and brought them together (through Moses) and made a covenant with them (on Mount Sinai); he identified himself with their concerns ('You will be my people and I will be your God'), and in return the people undertook to observe the law, 'the second commandment is like the first'. God involved himself in human history, and it is a history which is still going on today.

The Eternal involves himself with time, its slowness and its development. That is why the covenant must constantly be renewed, re-enacted. That is the *raison d'être* of the temple cult, and above all of the great gatherings which cannot be discussed in detail here, but which are well worth reading about once again: those on Sinai (Ex. 19; 24; 34); at Shechem (Josh. 24); and after the return from exile (Neh. 8; 9). In the Roman Missal this last passage can be found under the Third Sunday of Ordinary Time (Cycle C).

The new covenant: Jesus, the new Israel

When the time was accomplished, God committed himself to the uttermost in his covenant by sending his Son among us. Jesus is not a priest in the functional sense of the word; he was not a liturgical innovator (he was happy to celebrate the liturgy like any pious Jew), yet the Epistle to the Hebrews calls him the great high priest. He had no need of rites and sacrifices to celebrate the new covenant (when he instituted the eucharist, it was for our benefit). As the new Israel he gathered the people of God to himself; as the new Adam he is the whole of humankind. At the same time he is revelation, the living Word of God. And his sacrifice is his complete and perfect obedience to the Father's will. Nor was there any other gift by which the covenant could be sealed than his offering of himself on the cross.

Jesus was not a mountaineer who journeys on his way alone. He deliberately spoke of himself as the vine (a classical image of Israel) of which we are the branches; as the cornerstone of the new temple, of which we are the living stones; as the shepherd of the flock, of which we are the sheep. Jesus revealed himself as the universal gatherer together, and this was his main concern during the years of his ministry. He gathered the crowds together to teach them and show them, by his actions, the love of God; and above all he formed the group of the Twelve, the nucleus of the future Church.

It is significant that after the resurrection Jesus showed himself to the apostles when they were gathered together on the first day of the week (a Sunday assembly!).

God always works in the same way: in ancient times God had sought to reveal himself to a people; on this occasion it was in the Church that the Risen Christ was revealed. And it was to the Twelve, reunited on the day of Pentecost, that the Risen Christ sent his Holy Spirit, thus giving birth to the Church, whose calling is to gather all the nations together.

The Church, the new people of God

From this time onwards, the resurrection is no longer tied to the one country of Palestine nor to one particular moment in the history of humanity. The new Israel extends to cover the whole of humankind. The new people of God is the Church, the body of Christ extending over time and space, a body called to increase throughout history to the moment when the Son of Man will return to gather together all people of every nation, from every race and every culture.

The Church's mission is precisely that: to gather all people together. The Church must be true to the Master's word and at the same time 'teach all nations', so that men and women can respond to the universal covenant, 'that all may believe' and be saved. Like Jesus and with him the Church has to renew the covenant by being, like him, 'the body broken and the blood poured', and by being the means by which all humanity ascends towards God.

This is the Church's task: in remembrance of Jesus Christ to continue this worship which, already under the influence of the prophetic

Photo Rémy Tournus

movement in the Old Testament, became more and more spiritual to the point when, in Jesus, it became worship 'in spirit and in truth'.

But the Church, composed as it was of human beings, also needed liturgical worship. Like every human society, it experiences the overwhelming need to come together to celebrate.

And so the well-known phrase 'Do this in remembrance of me' can at the same time denote both the daily spiritual worship of the Church in spreading the gospel, teaching and giving its life, and also the celebration of what it experiences or seeks to experience daily in Jesus Christ.

25

A basic outline

From this short survey of the history of the covenant a basic scheme emerges clearly: its starting point is always the idea of gathering together, of meeting, of assembly. If you like, as well as the passages from the Old Testament which I have already mentioned, reread some texts from the New Testament in which many scholars think that they can find a liturgical structure: these include the Feeding of the Five Thousand (Matt. 14.15f.), the story of the travellers on the Road to Emmaus (Luke 24.13f.), the story of the Day of Pentecost (Luke 24.13f.) and the Epistle to the Hebrews (12.18–29).

God's plan always begins by gathering people together, hence the vital importance of the presence of an assembly at our celebrations.

And this assembly continually celebrates the events of the covenant by means of an exchange of words and symbolic actions.

And it was not just chance which led our Church to rediscover the priesthood of all believers.

In order to understand the liturgy, we shall spend some time on another discovery, linked to the first and given the blessing of Vatican II, that of the rediscovery of the assembly, the first and original liturgical sign, and the one which implies all the others. This rediscovery is far from being universally accepted, and we shall have occasion to stress the urgency of the change in attitudes that it entails.

8

Church and Assembly

It is only comparatively recently that the term 'assembly' has regained its place in liturgical vocabulary. For centuries, and sometimes even today, the term used has been the 'presence' of the faithful. Like all social groups, Christian circles have their jargon and their fashions. But in this case it is not just a matter of empty words: the rediscovery of the biblical and traditional term 'assembly' stands for the rediscovery of a reality of Christian faith.

Some vocabulary

In the Old Testament, the people assembled to renew the covenant: this gathering is called *qahal YHWH* in Hebrew, in English 'the assem-bly of God'. Intrinsic to the word *qahal* is the idea of calling together, convocation.

The Israelites were aware that they had not gathered of their own volition, but because God had called them, gathered them together. So when the Bible came to be translated into Greek (the Septuagint) it was quite natural for the word *qahal* to be rendered as *ekklesia* (from the Greek 'called out'). Latin used the same word, *ecclesia*, and this became *église* in French ('Church' in English has rather a different background, from the Greek *kyriake*, belonging to the Lord).

The Acts of the Apostles describes the early Christian communities as being assembled together 'in one place' and united 'in a single heart and mind'. In the same way it is significant that throughout the New Testament the term *ecclesia* is echoed in the expressions the Church of Christ, the Church of God, the Church of the Lord.

For us today this word Church stands for either the universal Church or, unfortunately, just the hierarchical and clerical part of it. Now it is clear that for the first Christians the word denoted the local Church: so the Book of Revelation is addressed to the 'seven Churches in Asia'. It is a good thing that this usage has come back today, and that without rejecting the classical use of the word which denotes the whole Church, one can talk not only of, say, the Church of England but of the Church in such and such a place.

To sum up, we need to remember the straight line which joins the term Church to the word assembly, so straight that the two words are virtual synonyms.

However, current usage has established a delicate distinction between Church and assembly. On the whole, Church tends to denote either the local group of Christians in a given place or the whole body of Christians scattered throughout the world. Assembly, on the other hand, is mainly used to denote a gathering of Christians in a given place at a given time. At this point we must add a third term, Sunday; we shall be reflecting later on the relationship between the three.

The assembly as the face of the Church

What appearance would the Church present without the assembly? Would it be a world-wide organization like UNESCO? A kind of freemasonry, intangible and yet infiltrating everything? The Church certainly makes its presence felt in a thousand ways (by the declaration of a national council of bishops, a journey made by the Pope, the Catholic press, Catholic Aid or CAFOD, a council, and so on). But it is the ordinary assembly, in a parish or elsewhere, which gives the Church its familiar everyday face. Let's not be naive about this: it will not be enough to hold high-powered liturgical gatherings which crowds flock to. The situation is more complex than that, since the foremost task of the Church and of every Christian is to bear witness to Jesus Christ and to spread his good news.

But what good will this be if the Church, both local and universal, shows a harsh face to the world through its assemblies? It is painful sometimes to watch people coming out of Mass with closed-up faces, or taking part in Masses whose sole aim seems to be to include as many collections as possible, or to find oneself in a Church where the worshippers seem to be playing at blind man's buff, to see gestures or objects which cannot be taken seriously, or to listen to words which are light-years away from real life. What good is it to spread the gospel if the Church (or the church building in which it is held) does not make one want to go inside? To be fair, one does sometimes have the pleasure of hearing someone talk of being helped a good deal from a particular service at a particular time, whether by chance or for reasons quite unconnected with the Church. Liturgical gatherings can bear witness either for or against the Church.

The face of the Church for Christians themselves

What would Christians make of the Church if there were no regular assemblies? Assemblies where they can not only be refreshed by the word and life of God, but also where they can feel the slightest vibration of the body of which they are members, and can be kept in touch with the apostolic mission to which they are called to lend their own unique support?

I know for a fact that many people today sincerely claim to be believers, while considering

Photo Rémy Tournus

it necessary to join only occasionally in congregational worship. No one can pass judgment on the faith of others. Yet what are we to think of someone who claims to belong to any kind of organization without ever taking part in its meetings or celebrations? At the very most one might call such a person a sympathizer.

The question which arises is this. There are many such 'sympathizers' in many countries. Is it that, preoccupied as they are with other concerns, they just do not bother to complain about tedious, routine and lifeless services? How many parents say to you, 'We are forced to belong to that particular parish because of our children. They can't bear going to Mass anywhere else'?

Those are some of the faces of assemblies, faces of the Church. And the responsibility does not lie solely with priests or those who arrange the liturgy: all of us, whoever we are, can cause this face either to smile or to frown. We shall be coming back to this in chapter 11.

In our reflections we have kept to a very human level of the importance of the assembly – I almost said its public or promotional level. Christians need to stand further back and remind themselves that the assembly is a mystery of faith. That is what the next chapter is about.

Christians, people who assemble

It is no coincidence that our age is rediscovering the assembly as an essential dimension of the Church.

The earliest Church defined Christians as people who assemble (in this connection look at the two passages in Acts on the first communities, in chapters 2 and 4). The pagan Pliny the Younger himself notes the importance of this fact in his letter to the emperor Trajan. We may also note that the term 'assemble' is one of the most frequent designations in the New Testament for what we now call a celebrating of the Mass.

When civil society and Church society came to coincide – a situation which is defined by the term Christendom – joining in the assembly was no more than a mark of Christian identity (even if everyone did not 'practise' regularly). The term assembly itself fell into disuse.

Similarly, the term Church no longer denoted the people of God but only its hierarchical structure; this language is so necessary that it has not died out. Finally, in the liturgical sphere, worship became the prerogative of the clergy.

But now our eyes have been opened. Christendom is dead and Christianity is a minority religion (even if many of our fellow-citizens may say that they are Christian). It is not surprising that this harsh awakening should go hand in hand with the rediscovery of mysteries conjured up by expressions like people of God, priesthood of the baptized and assembly. Besides, although the term does not say everything about him or her, for our contemporaries the Catholic is the one who goes to Mass. Whatever may be the ambiguity or the narrowness of such a criterion, the fact is there and should make us think.

Assemblies without a priest

In many dioceses, there are assemblies on Sunday without a priest. This gathering is based on the vital necessity for a local community to celebrate the Lord's Day together, where it is, whether or not there is the possibility of a eucharist.

For a long time, where local priests could not guarantee that there would be a eucharist, an appeal was made to others (for example, ordained teachers, and sometimes richer neighbouring dioceses). This was inconvenient, because since these people were strangers to the life of the local Church, there was a risk that the celebration would become disconnected from it. Later, there was an attempt to regroup Christians in a central parish; but it soon became clear that the absence of any meeting in the village church threatened to kill off Church life there.

That is why as a third stage, following the Council, services without priests were instituted in places where the social fabric (human and Christian) was sufficiently solid for the experiment to be viable. The sector priest would then come on certain Sundays to preside at a eucharist.

This practice derives its legitimacy from the liturgy, the link between assembly, Sunday and Church, and history: is this not the way in which the African Churches have existed since their foundation?

However, this should not become a facile solution to the question of presbyteral ministry and the negation of what some theologians call 'the right of Christians to the eucharist'.

These gatherings take the following pattern: opening rite, liturgy of the word, thanksgiving followed by an action which is often in fact communion. See the boxes in the chapters on the rites of the Mass.

9

The Assembly as a Sign of Faith

We are familiar with Paul's exhortation to the Corinthians about the eucharist: he told them to 'discern the body of the Lord', meaning by this not only the eucharistic bread but also the whole assembly of Christians at Corinth.

A document addressed to bishops in the third century (the *Didascalia*) makes this recommendation: 'Exhort the people to meet together faithfully. Let no one diminish the Church by his absence, so as not to diminish the body of Christ by one member.'

Seventeen centuries later, Vatican II affirmed in its Instruction on the Worship of the Eucharistic Mystery: 'The Church of Christ is truly present in all legitimate assemblies of the faithful which, united with their pastors, are called

Churches in the New Testament. These are, each in its own region, the new people, called by God in the Holy Spirit and in all fullness (I Thess. 1.5) . . . In these communities, though they may often be small or poor or living among the "Diaspora", Christ is present, by whose power the one holy, catholic and apostolic Church is united . . . He is always present in a body of the faithful gathered in his name' (*Eucharisticum Mysterium* 7, 9; cf. also 55).

So the believer is called to look upon the assembly as more than just itself. As we saw in the last chapter, the assembly is not only one of the visible faces of the Church; far more, in the eyes of faith it is a sign of a greater and invisible reality, the Church of Christ. The Church is invisible, because it brings together through time and space members whom we do not see, who are already with God, the saints and, on earth, those who seek God in integrity, the Church which we celebrate at All Saints' Tide, the Church which can be identified with the kingdom of God, which 'holds within it the fullness of Christ who himself receives the entire fullness of God' (Eph. 1.23), the body which is being built up so that we shall 'all at last attain to the unity inherent in our faith and our knowledge of the Son of God – to mature manhood, measured by nothing less than the full stature of Christ' (Eph. 4.13).

And so every single assembly of Christians, large or small, rich or poor in resources, is a manifestation of the body of Christ at a given place and a given time. *Lumen Gentium*, the Vatican II Constitution on the Church, affirms strongly that the assembly 'is, in Christ, a kind of sacrament of the Church', 'that is to say at the same time the sign and the means of intimate union with God and the unity of all the human race'.

In fact a sacrament is a sign which both explains an invisible reality and at the same time produces this invisible reality. We recognize in it the very action of the Saviour. And so it is God who brings us together, and the action of doing this is a sign of the Church and builds it up. Our assemblies join together to build up the Church of Christ.

But it is still necessary to be sure of the validity of the sign: is this particular assembly, this particular day, really a sign of the Church? The same goes for the seven sacraments. Too often

we are content just to go through the motions of performing the rite without trying to make it meaningful; here there is also a risk of dressing up an in-significant gathering in the name of a sacrament.

An assembly which is a sign

If it is to be a sign of the Church, if it is to be truly an assembly, a liturgical gathering must have these characteristics:
– it must be founded on the faith and have no other object than to celebrate the covenant of Jesus Christ:
– it must feel itself called together so that it can also be sent out to evangelize;
– it must be a gathering of brothers and sisters;
– it must be aware of being a chosen people, a holy people, in other words a people set apart, a people of those who are saved;
– it must celebrate in joy and hope.

If an assembly has these qualities, then it is truly able to be a sign of the kingdom which is to come but which has already begun, where in Jesus Christ God calls together all people, beyond the vicissitudes of our own personal and corporate histories, beyond suffering and death.

This is the programme which Luke describes in chapters 2 and 4 of the Acts of the Apostles. It is a fine programme, but we know that even in Paul's time it was far from being realized, and it seems rather idealistic when we look at the assemblies that we actually have.

There is a contradiction here, or rather a tension which is productive, and this we shall be looking at in more detail.

10

An Assembly under Tension

A liturgical assembly is original in that it is characterized by a series of qualities which are antonyms (see the table on page 34).

Sinners forgiven

The first of these antonyms is immediately obvious: calling to mind the First Letter of Peter (2.9), a preface reminds us that 'Christ called us to the glory that has made us a chosen race, a royal priesthood, a holy nation, a people set apart'. How pretentious and hypocritical this would be if, at the same time, the liturgy did not constantly remind us that we are a sinful people, 'stiff-necked and slow to be converted'!

United in diversity

Because of our human condition, our assemblies are necessarily limited. But at the same time they demand the gathering together of all people, without any distinction whatsoever. Assemblies in Paul's time were as diverse as they are today, and yet the apostle declared that 'there is neither Jew nor Greek, slave nor freeman, male nor female, for you are all one in Christ Jesus' (Gal. 3.28). Except in particular cases (see pages 41–2), the Christian assembly is by definition an open one – consisting of Christians on a journey – and aims to be pluralistic: in respect to cultures and epochs, social origins, religious sensibilities and political options, etc. In short, the people of God,

Deviations	Tensions		Deviations
moralism *culpabilism*	Sinners	. . . forgiven holy nation	*Church of the pure* *Pharisaism*
division	diversity	unity	*unanimism* *uniformity by fusion*
deterioration *of faith* *each one has his* *or her own* *religion*	weak believers	believers (faith of the Church)	*élitism*
activism *ideological action*	dispersion (mission)	gathering (celebration)	*sectarianism*
pessimism *despair*	trial	festival	*illuminism* *evasion, opium*
sectarianism	limited assembly	open gathering	*self-service* *anonymity*

Breach
through which God
can act

like any other group of people, is a varied and motley one. In normal circumstances the assembly should be seen to have the same profile as the society of which it is a product: we know that in many countries this is not the case and, as in other spheres, the working class is often virtually absent. The reason for this disaffection may more properly be looked for in the history of the Church than in the liturgy. All the same, this breach must be constantly felt and must necessarily have an effect on our assemblies.

And so, in the richness of this diversity, the assembly tries to be united 'with one heart and with one soul'. And we may go one stage further: an assembly's pluralism affects even its faith.

'I believe, Lord increase my faith'

One needs to have faith in order to take part in a Christian assembly. Otherwise, what meaning would the assembly have, and above all, what meaning could be given to its actions?

But what faith? When we recite the Nicene or the Apostles' Creed we are able to do so in all sincerity; but at the same time, think of the variation in ways of believing and even in the degree of faith that lies behind the words! And it is logical, when I come to a celebration of Mass, that I come not only to celebrate and affirm my faith in company with the whole Church, but also to nourish it by contact with the word of God and with my fellow Christians. 'I believe, Lord increase my faith.'

We believers are people on a journey. There are those who walk confidently and who are already well on the way (who? I don't know, but God does). There are those who drag their feet, either because they have been wounded by life or because they have not learned to walk properly. There are those who press forward eagerly and those who sometimes hang back. There are those driven by tremendous energy, and those who hesitate. But they are all people on the move, people showing their solidarity with one another both in grace and in sinfulness, in belief and in unbelief.

Gathered . . . and scattered

Above all today, Christians are scattered (in Diaspora, to use the classical term). Here they assemble, so that they can be separated from the world (a chosen people, a people set apart), not to remain in a cosy clique together ('Lord, it is good for us to be here; let us set up three tents') but to be sent into the world: 'Go in the peace of Christ', Go, teach, be witnesses . . . at your own risk and peril. 'You are not of the world, but I send you into the world.'

Evangelization – celebration – evangelization:

this sequence is the heartbeat of the Church: diastole, systole. Evangelization and celebrating the liturgy are two distinct things, but they are not in opposition: so much so that St Paul, in speaking of his apostolic mission, was able to use the language of the liturgy: 'By his gift of grace God has made me a minister of Christ to the Gentiles; my priestly service is the preaching of the gospel of God, and it falls to me to offer the Gentiles to him as an acceptable sacrifice, consecrated by the Holy Spirit' (Rom. 15.16).

A celebrating people

Gathered together in the faith, we are commanded to offer to God an act of thanksgiving for the great things he has done (in this sense, every Christian celebration is eucharistic, even outside the context of the Mass). We do not come to 'make merry', but our joy, which may be quiet and dignified, is the fruit by which the tree is recognized.

This is not a naive joy which forgets the cross inherent in human life or the drama of human existence. Who has not experienced this inner joy during a Christian funeral? A joy which is not morphine for grief, but which in some mysterious way dwells alongside it . . .

Necessary tensions

These contradictions are sometimes difficult to live with, and we all experience them to some extent. And yet we are not able to let go of either side of them without exposing our assemblies to deadly deviations. All these tensions are necessary.

It is tempting for a 'Church of the pure', which rejects those who are lukewarm, the 'bad Christians', to forget that we are a sinful people. This is to behave like the Pharisee. But if we forget that we are also a holy people, we lay ourselves open to blame, to the systematic cultivation of a bad conscience, to moralizing and in the end to a kind of spiritual masochism. We by no means always avoid this risk, and so we sterilize our Christian faith. In doing this we tend to forget that we are already saved by God. We have to hold on to the two terms: we are forgiven sinners (we shall be returning later to the subject of the act of penitence in the Mass – see page 96).

Encouraging divisions which cut across our assemblies would clearly be suicidal. Nevertheless they must be recognized and assimilated – a delicate task. Preachers are well aware that one word, a single unfortunate word, can provoke a protest: 'We come here to be united, and you divide us.' This is a protest which often conceals a desire for a false unity, one which buries differences: in a word, not unity but uniformity. People behave as if the whole world should think and live in the same way. That is not the way to true unity. The real path is the one of reconciliation.

Reconciliation is to be sought in every aspect of life: in tolerance towards those who do not pray as I do, those who do not believe as I do, those who do not like the music I do, who do not vote as I do.

We need to keep the balance between unity and diversity!

We are people gathered together to celebrate, people sent out to evangelize. To abandon either of these two extremes would be a mortal danger for the Church, a serious betrayal of its calling.

To put evangelization first at the expense of worship is to risk seeing the apostolic task degenerate into an activity severed from its spiritual roots; going to the extremes of missionary activity is not going to build up and augment the body of Christ.

On the other hand, an assembly which has lost its impetus to evangelize can justly be reproached for escaping into the sacred, or for seeking a cosy religion. Having faith means taking risks, and evangelization is vital.

Our assemblies are defined, but are always open. If they are not always open to all types of believers, they run the risk of being considered élitist, and are seen to degenerate into sects. But if they are open to the point of indulging religious individualism, our celebrations will become a self-service cafeteria in which each person can choose his or her own plate of spiritual food without regard for anyone else.

Finally, Christian joy was not bought without cost. It is Easter joy, and before the resurrection came Gethsemane. If it does not take seriously the deep tragedy of Christian and human existence, the joy of our assemblies will turn to illuminism.

Gathering together is a prophetic act

In the end of the day these tensions mirror our Christian lives and the story of salvation. Nothing stands still, everything is always moving on. Everything has been accomplished by the blood shed on the cross but at the same time there is still everything to do. Everything has been given already; everything is still to be received.

And so gathering together is a prophetic act which reveals God and makes his promise known. When we meet together we affirm that God has already shared his holiness with us, but in letting ourselves be converted by his word we are gambling on the promises he has made us that we shall beyond all doubt share in his happiness. By shedding his blood on the cross, Christ Jesus has bought a people for himself, but this people has to grow to the whole stature of Christ himself, and when we assemble – whether it is in groups of twenty or a thousand, we are gambling on this universal assembling. We are one in Christ, but through our very differences, we are gambling on this unity which our Saviour has given us, and our desire is to be instruments of peace. Christ brings us together, but we accept the fact that he sends us out, because 'there are other sheep, which are not of this fold'. Faith brings us together, and through faith we also confess a God who seeks, a holy God whom we cannot touch, and we gamble on the hope of seeing him one day as he is. That is hope and joy.

Our assemblies, marking out both the life of the Church and our own personal lives, are important landmarks in our faith and hope; from one service of worship to the next, we are hastening on the day of his return and the coming of his kingdom.

Masses in small groups

It is good, legitimate and desirable that groups of Christians who gather together out of like-mindedness or out of a precise apostolic motivation or for some pedagogical reason should also gather together to celebrate. Clearly the gathering is no longer open. However, it must remain at least potentially so, and show that it is in communion with pluralist gatherings. The priest's specific role is to remind them constantly of this link with 'catholicity', in other words with the universal Church.

Masses with children and young people

Terms like this are questionable. Basically there is only the Mass of the people of God, and in a children's Mass there are always some adults, if only the priest; these remind us in passing that we are not making children celebrate but celebrating with them.

On the other hand it is wrong to reject this practice as being illegitimate where an attempt is being made to adapt the celebration to the psychology, the sensibility and the spiritual development of young people without making the gospel infantile. Thank God we are now discovering the vital place of symbolic action in training in the faith.

However, the considerable effort made in this area leaves open the question of the participation of children and young people in regular services. For if they only celebrate by themselves, there is a risk of forming a parallel Church, a risk that they will never be integrated into the grown-up Church, in short that they will leave the Church entirely, saying, like so many others, that it is something for kids.

So in parish Masses, questions need to be asked:

Are children looked after by grown-ups (not just those who are more specifically in charge of them) or are they left to themselves?

Are they allowed to play any part in the service? At this age, doing something is the best way of joining in. We need to be inventive in giving young people tasks in the new pattern of ritual; one can assign them certain services to perform like the reading, as long as they prepare it, or bringing the bread and wine to the altar.

How can one encourage them to participate? In the liturgy, does their presence count or is more attention paid to the old Christians whose habits there is a reluctance to disturb?

More suggestions for Masses with young people can be found in Edward Matthews, *Celebrating Mass with Children*, Collins Liturgical Publications 1975.

11

Everyone Bears Responsibility

'It is the assembly itself which celebrates the eucharist.' Even today, some people find such a statement astonishing. However, it is taken from a document put out by the French bishops on which I am going to draw heavily in the following pages (*Tous responsables dans l'Eglise?*, Editions du Centurion 1973).

The statement is based on the idea of priesthood by baptism which is now fairly familiar in the Church and which has taken concrete shape, for instance, in the Catholic Action movement in France. The whole body of the Church has an obligation to carry on the work of Christ. Our baptism has made us members of Christ, the king, priest and prophet. As king, Christ came to gather all humankind into his father's kingdom; as priest, he is the perfect intermediary between God and humanity; as prophet, he is the living word of God. We must understand that the task of spreading the gospel is no longer just 'the

priest's job', to speak colloquially. All of us are called by our baptism to be witnesses to the gospel, to gather people together and serve them by working for peace and justice and by freeing them from all that alienates them.

But isn't the liturgy still too often just 'the priest's job'? True, a significant number of Christians are interested in the liturgy and do contribute towards it. But sometimes the way in which they talk about what they do betrays the fact that they see themselves as 'helping the priest'. The ready willingness which they show in preparing and indeed taking part in forms of worship is a great hope for the Church of tomorrow.

In doing this they are not acting as 'spare wheels' to clergy in the process of decline, but are quite simply both carrying out their duty and claiming their right as baptized persons.

This is a complete U-turn in which all the

people of God are invited to take part. As a priestly people, they have an obligation to continue the world-offering which Jesus made on the cross, through their Christian life and also through their worship.

It is important to be clear about this. In affirming the assembly's prerogative there is no question of denying the indispensability of ministries, especially that of the priest, who has a specific role.

In order to survive, the assembly needs ministries and services. Any human group needs these to function: there must be a president (or leader), secretaries, people to supervise what needs to be done.

That is even more true of the Church, where the Holy Spirit inspires all the gifts which are needed in building up the Body of Christ, both in worship and in the world.

The assembly bears responsibility for itself, and those who exercise a ministry within the assembly are at its service (that is in fact the meaning of the word ministry). This service assumes a power (for example, a capacity to speak in public, or to communicate, or to organize things). But ministers are human and there is always the big temptation – albeit an unconscious one – for them to abuse the power they have, particularly when they have behind them centuries of clerical domination when, as the saying had it, 'sheep are only good for being shorn', and the people were only there to say Amen.

What we need to do is to enable the assembly to express its own soul and not that of the minister. The assembly must not be manipulated. An assembly has to be made into a community, without forgetting that it is composed of individual people. There are particular roles in the Church, indeed a hierarchy, but they must not extinguish the workings of the Spirit (here are two more fruitful sources of tension in addition to the ones that I listed on page 34).

There is no question here of putting priest and leaders on trial. To be fair, it must be said that the faithful often show a disarming passivity. What do adults do when a child is left to itself and creates havoc? What do they do when there is a small child next to them who is unsuccessfully looking for the hymn in his hymnbook? And when a drunk comes into church, isn't it the priest himself who has so often to show him out?

Photo Rémy Tournus

Photo Rémy Tournus

Watch, next Sunday.

We need, little by little, to create conditions which encourage this sense of responsibility on the part of the assembly (over and above participation in worship). On the occasion of 'first communions', shouldn't all practising Christians be invited to participate, in spite of the crowds that may result, so that the families are in contact with a genuine, living assembly? When, on Easter Eve, someone (often quite an elderly person) says, 'I know that this question may make you laugh, but what really counts tomorrow?', the answer should be, 'Can the others count on you?' (The implication is that those people who only come to make their Easter communion need the regular assembly.)

Those are fortunate assemblies whose members do not want to be absent so that they shall not, to use the old expression, 'diminish the body of Christ', and so play their part, however modest it may be, in praying and singing.

Without an assembly there can be no liturgy. The Church has always recognized the validity of a eucharist celebrated by the priest alone because by his ordination he is the representative of the Church. But we must understand in

A word which has no equivalent in English

We have only one word in English to translate two Greek words which are used in the New Testament. In practice we use the word priest for both *hiereus* and *presbyteros* – and that is extremely inconvenient.

Christ is called *hiereus* because he is the perfect mediator between God and humanity. This term is used in pagan religions for those who have the power of direct access to the divine.

In Jesus Christ, the whole Church today continues his task of being the one *hiereus*. That is why St Peter tells us that we are a priestly nation.

On the other hand the term *presbyteros* (which means 'elder' and which has given us our word 'priest') denotes the officials who lead the community.

In spite of the well-known phrase, we are not a 'people of priests' any more than Christ was a presbyter. But all of us together have the task of carrying out the work of Christ, 'the high priest', and the task of those who are bishops and priests is to make sure that we are faithful.

Photo Rémy Tournus

Sisters of St Paul of Kinshasa. *Photo E.P.A.*

Words which betray us

'At what time do you say your Mass, please?'
'My friend, in the first place it is not my Mass. And secondly, I do not say it; we celebrate it together.'

'Good morning, Father, I've come to bring flowers for your church (or, for your sick people).'
'That's very kind of you, Mrs X. But just between ourselves, they are not for my church but for our church (our sick).'

Seen in a Catholic journal (unfortunately a recent one): 'On the occasion of his jubilee Mgr X will concelebrate High Mass at 10 a.m. in the cathedral of Y with the priests of his year. The choir will perform (the programme follows) and Maestro Z, the organist, will play the following works (. . . again the programme). We hope that many people will be present to support the celebrations.'

'Celebrant' is a term which we often use to denote the priest who presides at the eucharist. Yet we are all celebrants, or better concelebrants. But the new term 'president' does sound rather strange. What we need is a term which conveys the idea of giving a service to the assembly.

If the assembly is the first sign

If the assembly is the first sign of the Christian liturgy, what must we do to make this sign meaningful?

Here are some questions which should be asked before any act of worship:

Does the place of worship, its decorations, lighting and acoustics, assist the assembly? (see chapter 18). Many churches are now too big for assemblies which are too small; does the place serve the assembly or the assembly the place?

A question linked to the previous one: at what time are Masses held?

Out of a desire to be of service, and for practical reasons, but also through motives which I suspect are less noble, the number of Masses has been unduly increased, at least in towns (I know of one where five central parishes have two Saturday Masses in anticipation!). The result is that, instead of coming together, the people separate.

One problem that is worth studying, both in town and country, is whether the policy adopted in holding services makes for a meaningful assembly or an individualistic, 'self-service' approach.

the light of all the gifts of the New Testament and the earliest tradition that this kind of celebration is not natural. (That is why the eucharistic ritual requires that, except in an emergency, there should be at least one minister.)

By its very nature, liturgy presupposes the participation of an assembly. And every pastoral effort should be made to fight against the 'privatization of the sacraments'; each time that the circle can be extended, by a baptism, administration of communion to the sick or even the sacrament of reconciliation, the Church has been made to grow.

12

At the Service of the Assembly

'The assembly as it is is the subject of the eucharistic celebration,' said the document from the French bishops which I mentioned in the previous chapter.

It went on: 'Everyone plays his or her role in it: some bring gifts, others read scripture, explain it for their brothers and sisters or share in it in a brotherly way . . . There can and must be a sharing of functions here, all the more since, in the past, historical circumstances have led to a concentration of powers in the hands of the priest or the bishop. But it is the specific role of the one who represents the Christ-shepherd among his brothers and sisters to proclaim the gospel and invoke the Holy Spirit "over the assembly and its gifts" (*epiclesis*) in the eucharistic prayer so that Christ may be made present to us and we may share his body and his blood.

It is the same faithful Christian who, by virtue of ordination, takes pastoral charge of the Church community as such and who exercises the ministry of presiding over the eucharistic assembly. Besides, it must never be forgotten that the very nature of this celebration requires that this organic diversification of functions should take place in a climate of welcome and brotherly sharing (cf. I Cor. 11.17–34; 13).'

The biblical image of the flock by itself would be a misleading one to use for the Church or the assembly. Another image needs to be added: that of an organic, structured body in which the members have different functions and are at the same time in solidarity with them. This is the well-known comparison that Paul uses (in I Cor. 12), precisely when he is called upon to impose some clear thinking and order on the community of the Corinthians, who seem to him to have run rather wild.

Ministries and services

Even in our time, our bishops have felt it necessary to draw distinctions in a vocabulary which is rather flexible.

'Ministry' and 'service' are two terms which translate the ancient Greek word *diakonia* (from which deacon comes). In the document quoted above the bishops want to reserve the word ministry for those functions which have the following five characteristics:

– a clearly defined service, for example teaching the catechism in a school or the pastoral care of the sick in hospitals;

– a service of vital importance for the life of the Church:

– a service which carries real responsibility: the minister 'assumes a charge before the Church of God and therefore before Christ and his Holy Spirit';

– a service recognized by the local Church through a liturgical act or merely by nomination;

– a service which has some degree of permanence (this is left rather vague).

Ministries and services exist in all areas of the Church's activity, and certainly also in the liturgy. Presiding at the eucharist, preaching the word, welcoming people, distributing communion, leading the singing, playing an instrument, singing a psalm, taking the collection – these are all ministries and services, so much so that we shall be examining each one in connection with the rite with which it is most concerned. The ministry of the priest (or president) calls for a separate study, because it is a key position.

Meanwhile it might be useful to define the spirit in which each function must be carried out and what qualities it may require: a spirit of service, faith, competence and a team spirit.

A spirit of service

A certain amount of power necessarily goes with service at the heart of the assembly. This is power received from the hands of the bishop at ordination, or at least power which depends on the competence and trust accorded to such a person.

But anyone who exercises power in an assembly ought always to remember the word of the one who 'came to minister and not be ministered to'. In practice, as far as the priest is concerned, this means that he does not 'pontificate' to or manipulate the assembly; those who lead worship must respect the assembly; and the choirmaster must not impose his own tastes.

Faith

Tradition has always insisted that the performance of liturgical ministries and services should not be entrusted to anyone whose life was not free from scandal. This situation was not always avoided during the time when most services were paid for and thought of as any other job. It is altogether different in our day.

It is true that a Christian who performs a ministry or service, even including the priest himself, is not only a sinner like everyone else but is not protected from experiencing difficulties in belief or lack of faith. But anyone who holds liturgical office is required above all to seek in the liturgy what is the faith of the Church, even in the midst of a personal crisis.

At all events, one cannot but wish for and encourage every effort made to ensure that those who undertake these functions can cope with the consequences in their personal lives.

Competence

Doing something means doing it competently. Each service must be performed with technical competence (for example, a reader must know how to read aloud; an organist must have mastered the art of accompanying) and also with liturgical competence.

The Constitution on the Sacred Liturgy says: 'They must all be deeply imbued with the spirit of the liturgy, each in his own measure, and they must be trained to perform their functions in a correct and orderly manner' (29).

The liturgical movement which has developed

Sisters of St Paul of Kinshasa. *Photo E.P.A.*

in recent decades has stimulated an enormous amount of good will. But here again, is good will enough? When priests do not know how to celebrate because they have only learned 'to say Mass', when cantors sing badly or out of tune, when lessons are read by people who do not understand the word they are proclaiming, when organists are totally ignorant of the laws of liturgy . . . We should have the courage to recognize the fact: despite an enormous amount of good will, the result is often very disappointing.

Do not think that I am being a purist in making comments like this. I realize, too, that we need time: the Church was not built in a day. Technical faults can readily be overlooked if the liturgy is truly celebrated. And one knows that it is natural to launch into a ministry and then, with some experience, realize that there is a need to acquire more competence. The time has come for being firm with those who undertake a ministry of service; the situation is a serious one.

A spirit of dialogue

If the assembly and the liturgy which it performs

Training

Many people already undergo some form of training, by taking part in either a session or a series of evenings or weekends, or by regularly reading a specialist journal. The task is immense: little by little a training network is being built up, at both regional and diocesan levels and even in sectors. Interested readers should know that in almost every diocese there is someone responsible for liturgy and liturgical music who can tell them what training is available.

are mysteries of communion, it goes without saying that one expects a comradely spirit among the various people involved in celebration.

This kindred spirit, I was almost going to say complicity, is necessary not only to 'oil the wheels' but also as witness. That is unquestionably the significance of the reaction that one sometimes hears when coming out of a Mass: 'In your Church we feel that there's a team.' This is a testimony to a community sense which reacts

44

upon the communion within the assembly itself.

Leaving aside quarrels over who is to read, or the little nastinesses that can go with them (as we unfortunately find), it has to be acknowledged that when people want to do well they easily get irritated at other people's mistakes. That's human. Here's a classic example. The organist has mistimed his interlude. There are two possible attitudes: the priest at the altar can gaze at the organ console sighing, with a black look (it's marvellous when he doesn't actually interrupt the music), and communicate his irritation and his annoyance to the assembly. Alternatively, when everyone realizes that the music is going on too long, the priest has only to give a small understanding smile to the congregation, and the day is saved.

It is not possible to have a successful celebration unless everyone respects one another, and a certain amount of agreement has been reached over the service beforehand.

Being a participant before being a minister

'I'm a bishop for you and a Christian with you,' said St Augustine. One might rephrase this: a minister for you, a member of the assembly with you.

In other words, the priest's role at the celebration is not just to lead prayer, see that the word is heard, and offer the eucharist; the cantor is not there just to help others to sing; the reader is not there just to proclaim the word; in company with all the baptized we, I, pray, listen, offer and communicate.

The preoccupations that go with our office can often make us forget this. We must be on our guard; otherwise, we run the risk of being involved in unedifying scenes: for example, a priest at the penitential rite giving the impression of no longer being concerned once the Kyrie begins. While everyone is listening to the word he summons a choirboy for goodness knows what . . . or puts the pages of his sermon in order. While everyone is singing a meditative psalm he is already on his way to the ambo (for fear of being late?). At the end of the preface he invites the congregation to sing the Sanctus with one voice – and he is turning over the pages of his missal, backwards and forwards, to find the eucharistic prayer (if only he had put a marker in!). The girl reader has just finished saying the general intercessions and while the priest brings it to an end she goes back to her place – heels clicking. The Gloria has been sung, and during the priest's prayer the leader fidgets with his lectern or with his music . . . One could find many more examples.

Even worse, one often gets the impression (I say impression, but in liturgy impressions are more powerful than intentions) that the priest is saying or reading prayers but that he is not praying as he says them.

A reflection of the assembly

By taking part, we help real participation. The role of ministers puts them in full view of the congregation, above all now that the Mass is celebrated facing the people. The architecture of most of our churches emphasizes this situation even more; seeing virtually nothing except other people's backs, the members of the congregation see the faces only of the priest and some other ministers in the choir. So we are the reflection of the assembly, and our bearing has a great effect on the attitude of people in it. In time past, pious people could often be heard to exclaim: 'Oh, Father X, he's a saint. I do so enjoy going to his Mass.' In other words, he prayed himself, and so helped others to pray. Since the time of Vatican II, this kind of expectation has never been so true.

13

Presiding

Everything I have said so far about those who are responsible for ministries and offices in the assembly holds good for the person who presides at the eucharist.

Preside means, etymologically, 'be seated in front of'. If in our language the word has unfortunate connotations, we should remember that on the occasion when he 'presided' at the Last Supper, Jesus made himself a slave, a domestic servant, by washing his friends' feet.

Among the ministries, those of bishop and priest are of paramount importance for Catholics. The episcopal document I have already quoted explains things like this:

'It is not primarily for organizational reasons but to signify and actualize the initiative and presence of Christ in the assembly, to ensure the unity of the particular Church, its communion with the other Churches, in the universal Church, and the continuity of the apostolic mission, that some of these brothers receive the charge of the pastoral ministry (bishop or priest) and preside at the eucharist.

"The minister shows that the assembly does not own the action that it is in process of performing; that it is not mistress of the eucharist. It receives the eucharist from another, Christ living in his Church. While remaining a member of the assembly, the minister is also the delegate who signifies the divine initiative and the link between the local community and the other communities in the universal Church" (Dombes Group, *Vers une meme foi eucharistique?*, 1972, no. 34).

It is above all within the framework of the celebration of the remembrance of the Lord that bishops and priests exercise the cultural and doxological function which comprises their ministry, though their ministry cannot be reduced to that.'

The General Instruction of the Roman Missal defines the role of the priest presiding at the eucharist in this way, in a few lines which we shall examine one by one.

'At the head of the assembly, as if taking Christ's place . . .'

Let us recall the Pauline comparison of the body of which Christ is the head. The assembly has a head, Christ, whose presence is symbolized by the presiding minister. The priest is a member of the assembly, and his role is to signify the presence of Christ (see GIRM 60).

So the priest takes the role of Christ, not in the theatrical sense of the word, but by identifying himself, as far as he can, with the one whose place he symbolically holds.

But he remains himself. His important role does not mean that he has to shut himself up in his priestliness, frozen and at a distance. He retains all his humanity, with his own qualities and charisms and his capacity for being close to the congregation; and his own limitations, too.

But at the same time as he allows himself to be invested with his role, he tries to be transparent to the active presence of the one who is the true head: 'By his actions and by his proclamations of the word he should impress upon the faithful the living presence of Christ' (GIRM 60).

'. . . he presides over prayer'

This statement is primarily about eucharistic prayer, which we will come back to again later (on page 132), and the 'presidential prayers' which used to be called collects ('gather up'), that form the general conclusion to the main part of the service (the opening, offertory, communion, for example). In this way the priest 'addresses God in the name of all the holy people'.

It must be said that in practice these prayers are often not very effective as a means of communication. There are perhaps two reasons for this, which are connected: the way they are said and the wording suggested by the missal.

For instance, how can one say this prayer after communion for the Thirtieth Sunday of Year C:

> Lord,
> bring to perfection within us
> the communion we share in this sacrament.
> May our celebration have an effect in our lives.

It would be a marvellous exercise in sacramental theology to meditate on these words at home, book in hand, but they are certainly not a prayer to be offered for and in the name of the people.

Here we come up against a weakness of the Roman Missal. At least to start with, those responsible for it were content to translate the ancient treasure house of collects, but it very soon became evident that they no longer speak to us. Their Latin precision, their complicated syntax, their theological conceptions so far removed from our contemporary world, their inappropriate language can only be of interest now to students of liturgy. One has only to compare them with the new second-generation prayers (for example in votive Masses, funerals and services of reconciliation).

Besides, the prayers bear no relation to the mystery celebrated on the day. On the same Thirtieth Sunday in Year C the Gospel reading is about the Pharisee and the Publican and the opening prayer is that God may 'strengthen our faith, hope and love'. The wish expressed by the ritual that 'the opening prayer should express the theme of the celebration' (GIRM 32) has not therefore been fulfilled.

In broader terms, presiding over prayer means helping people to pray. And I would like to say that all methods are good ones: after the communion, if there is no hymn, is there anything against saying the prayer slowly, with pauses, in a very intimate way, as if slipping into an attitude of prayer that is almost second nature, as one would naturally use for children? Perhaps presiding at prayer isn't just a matter of being satisfied with the prayers in the Missal; there is nothing against adding a prayer to a psalm or a reading when pastoral concerns make it advisable. There are some lovely prayers in the ecumenical psalter, or in some popular missals.

Presiding at prayer also means introducing certain corporate prayers: 'I confess to God', 'Our

Master of Westphalia. *Photo Giraudon*

Father', and so on. The quality of the act of prayer will depend on the way we do this: it can be either a recited formula or a true prayer.

To sum up, presiding at prayer amounts to setting the tone, whether it be one of inwardness, praise, adoration, contemplation, meditation and so on.

. . . 'He preaches the message of salvation'

'The homily should ordinarily be given by the celebrant' (GIRM 42). See chapter 25.

. . . 'He joins with the people in the sacrifice of Christ'

This question has already been raised in chapter 6, and we shall be returning to it in connection with the eucharist.

'Like the hostess . . .'

Like the hostess, the president of the assembly sees that everything is ready for the celebration (the setting, the utensils, the order of service, the sharing of duties). Why should he not also welcome people at the door, too, before going to take his place, instead of entering hieratically in a procession? It is also important for him to pay attention to each individual and each group of people, making them welcome and making others aware of their presence. In a word, he welcomes them in the name of the Lord and helps them to welcome one another. In addition to other things, the priest is the link-man.

He is the link between people (before, during and after the service). He is the link between the sections of the celebration. Just as the host or hostess determines the pattern of a party, timing the meal, when the next course is to be brought in, producing the birthday cake, proposing toasts, so the president controls the different parts of the celebration and helps the worshippers to make the connection between them, to grasp their dynamics and their profound unity. He does this less by giving a running commentary than by the intelligent way in which he celebrates (for example making use of a preceding hymn to introduce a prayer). Why not, for example, pick up the words of the opening hymn in the sentence of welcome, the penitential prayer or the concluding prayer? Again this means that he has to know what is being sung. It is worth repeating that liturgy is teamwork.

He is a link between the different ministries and offices. 'Each person, minister or layman, who has an office to perform, should carry out *all and only* those parts which pertain to his office' (*Constitution on the Liturgy*, my emphasis). I have already said that the priest is not the factotum of the liturgy. But he is the one who harmonizes the roles of those taking part. It is thanks to him that each individual can put to use 'the varied gifts of the Spirit'.

Certainly, there are small congregations with limited resources. Are they also as spiritually poor as might be supposed? Services on Sundays where no priest is present enable people to discover talents they did not know that they had.

Perhaps the presence of a priest prevents them from discovering these?

In the end it is up to the president to encourage the timid reader, to check a commentator who is too talkative or a choir which is too exuberant, to help the organist to have the right role . . .

He is the link between the celebration and everyday life. The hostess asks those whom she invites how they are. The priest will normally do this when making his pastoral visits. But a welcome at the church door could also have an important role to play, and be a good focus for the ritual of welcome.

He is the link between an individual assembly and the Church universal. This is really his true role, the one he holds from the bishop, who is himself responsible to the whole Church. This task is still more important when the celebration is limited to a particular group.

He is the link between the assembly and 'he who comes'. As president of the assembly, the priest takes his bearings from the future, from the world to come. As a symbol of the Christ who was sent by the Father and who returns to the Father, he reminds believers that everything is given from above and that everything has to return to God, through the one who has gone before us to lead us towards the kingdom.

As in the liturgy so in the life of the Church

The lay person reading this may think that I have written too much on the subject of the priest as president of the assembly. That is his primary function, as I have said, but we must realize that the pastoral ministry is too important to be glossed over.

It is essential to get the liturgical role of the priest into focus, since its characteristics are also found in the life of the Church. As in the liturgy, he is the lynch pin who makes the link between people, between groups, between Church activities (mission, teaching, charity work and so on),

between all of these and God. He is the driving force or, if you prefer, the active watchman, sharing here in the charge given by his bishop.

Mass the wrong way round?

In former times, both priest and worshippers faced the same way, like a procession en route to another place. There was meaning in this, and it was with some justification that Claudel criticized 'Mass the wrong way round'.

It would be serious if a Mass celebrated facing the people excluded this dimension of 'another place'. One could perhaps indicate that dimension, for example, by turning to the cross when making the sign of the cross with the congregation. But the most important consideration here is where the priest is looking.

'Don't look at the worshippers when you face them,' one used to be told in earlier times. But when a priest celebrates today facing the people, it is so that he can communicate with them more easily. So he should know how to look the congregation in the eye, at the peace, the admonitions, the homily, the final blessing.

On the other hand, when saying a prayer, he can change the focus towards another place: by raising his eyes to heaven or closing his eyes. It is up to everyone to find his own means of expression.

Assemblies without a priest

Many lay people refuse to preside over an assembly without a priest, instinctively shrinking from 'playing' at being a priest. Often, when there are presidents, the preference is for a collegial celebration.

It would certainly be sad if services without a priest became the occasion for a neo-clericalism: if the factotum clergyman were succeeded by a lay man or woman who monopolized the service. More than ever the situation calls for the widest possible sharing of ministries and offices.

However, many lay people feel the need to be recognized by the bishop or those in authority under him, not out of ambition, but so that their responsibility has a real place in a wider mission.

14

From Words to Actions

In the beginning was the word

The word holds an important place in Christianity. On reading the Bible, we see that:

The word was present at Creation (Gen. 1; Ps. 33.6). Moreover, in Hebrew the word *dabar* means to create as well as to speak: 'God spoke, and there was light.' We see by this how effective speech can be (performative)!

After speaking through the prophets, God spoke through Jesus, his living Word, not only in the words which he uttered, but also by his life.

By his resurrection, he gave us the Holy Spirit, 'who will speak of the things to come' (John 16.13).

In turn he sent us, 'Go, teach all nations' (Matt. 18–20).

And those who receive his word let themselves be transformed by the 'enduring word of God' (I Peter 1.13).

'In the beginning was the Word' – and the whole history of salvation, the whole development of the Church, all Christian life from its beginning through the centuries, is marked out by the word of God.

Stages in the history of the word

1. The Second Vatican Council reminded us that 'God is not far from those who seek him', even in ignorance, and that in a mysterious way God speaks with them as he did with Abraham. And *Lumen Gentium* sees here 'a preparation for the gospel'.

2. Evangelism is the proclamation of Jesus Christ as Saviour with a view to converting people to the faith.

3. Catechetical instruction is offered world-wide to those who have accepted the good news, whose aim is to deepen the faith and illuminate it by doctrine. In Church, the scriptures are inter-

preted to them.

4. The sacrament. At the head comes baptism, as a seal of the faith.

5. The Christian life. Transformed by faith, the Christian lives his life in imitation of Christ and becomes his witness. Those are the 'fruits' of the word.

Let us simplify things a little:
In the first place, a word is given and received;
then a word is celebrated;
finally a word is lived.

In his book *Symbolique et Symbole*, published by Editions du Cerf, L. M. Chauvet – to whom I owe the broad outline of the opening of this chapter – suggests the following reading, among others, of the story of the disciples on the Emmaus road.

	The disciples, turning their backs on Jerusalem, told Jesus of their confusion and of the recent happenings. But their eyes were still shut; they did not see the significance of them. They could see no meaning.
Word given and received	Jesus explained the scriptures to them, and they still did not understand. But a glimmer of light appeared: 'Stay with us, sir' (a sign that the word had been received). Their faith began to develop.
Word celebrated	It is in the breaking of the bread that the word becomes action or, as we would say, sacrament. Then 'their eyes were opened'. But Jesus disappeared from their sight; present in the celebration, he becomes the absent one.
Word lived	They cannot find him again except by going to their brothers and sisters, returning (conversion) to Jerusalem; this is the faith lived out in the Church, shared and verified. 'It is true . . . he has appeared also to Simon.'

The word celebrated

This reading shows clearly how the word celebrated links up with evangelism and a moral life. It is also a perfect illustration of the close connection there is between word and sacrament.

It is not only that the proclamation of the word comes before the sacrament, but at the heart of any sacrament there is always a liturgy of the word.

Not only does sacramentalization succeed evangelization chronologically, but there is also a very close link between the two. Did you notice in the story of the Emmaus road that it was the action of breaking bread which 'opened the eyes' of the disciples? In other words, evangelization is wholly truthful only in the context of the sacrament. Conversely, it would be attributing a magic power to the sacrament if one celebrated it with those who did not know enough of the gospel.

Evangelization, celebration and the Christian life of witness are three links in the same chain. To take another example: young Christian couples preparing for marriage, during their instruction or because they have had a Catholic upbringing, already discover that their love is a sign of God's covenant, but they only realize the full force and truth of this in the celebration of the sacrament. And the third stage is that all their married life is illuminated by the sacrament, which they try to live out in their daily lives.

From the word to the saving action

In all our liturgy, we are celebrating first of all the word in order to remind ourselves of God's action, to extend and deepen the spread of the gospel of which we are the recipients as well as the agents, and to formulate our faith; in short we let ourselves be invested and transformed by what is already a memorial of the covenant.

In his Church, the word takes substance and

The disciples at Emmaus. Thirteenth century. Bourget church. *Photo Rémy Tournus*

becomes the saving action of Jesus Christ.

The liturgy of the word says that Christ was offered for us. And the eucharistic action renews the offering of Christ. 'Christ died and is risen again.' The person who is baptized immerses himself or herself in the mystery of Easter. The word of God makes him a member of the body of Christ. 'God has sealed a covenant with us,' says the liturgy of the word. The word of Christ makes the consent of husband and wife a mystical reality, a sacrament of the new covenant. And so on.

The word of God becomes action. Saying is doing.

Sacramental words

There is never a sacramental action without sacramental words. These are what lie at the heart of the rite: words of consecration, absolution, baptism.

In the first place words are there to make the meaning of the action absolutely clear. For example, we are baptized 'in the name of the Father, of the Son and of the Holy Spirit'. In fact this action is not peculiar to Christians. Ritual bathing takes place in many religions.

But above all words are there because the sacraments are the work of Christ, the effective Word of God.

Sacramental actions

And in the sacraments there can be no word without actions, for the reasons that we considered earlier. The action is symbolic.

Someone may object that in the confessional the words of absolution are enough. That is true; but it is not the usual form. This exception is proof that, in the sacrament, the word is itself an action.

Everything that has been said about symbol and ritual ought to help in our understanding of the liturgy from within, but that is not the whole story.

What is specific to Christian liturgy must be shown: in other words, the four pillars of the assembly, the president, the word and the action.

Before we look at each sacrament individually, we must first of all examine the various aspects of the way in which a celebration takes place by examining some of the components.

53

15

Communication within the Assembly

In fact, the whole liturgy is word.

First of all there is the Word of God, and specifically liturgical words.

This word of God also turns into an act of prayer (the prayers of the president or the prayers of the assembly).

There are the words which structure the assembly (greetings, dialogues).

In addition, there are the words which accompany the ritual in order to emphasize its meaning: 'Behold the lamb of God . . .' 'This is the word of the Lord': those which introduce rites: 'Let us pray . . .', 'Let us give thanks to the Lord our God'.

There are words which are in the nature of a homily (the introductory matter to readings).

The liturgy, too, is a means of communication. For those who play a particular role in the assembly, it is an art-form whose rules they have to learn.

Listen, listen

Throughout its history the Church has favoured listening, listening to the revealed word of God and the words of prayer which, in the early centuries, the assembly interrupted with acclamations and short responses. Unfortunately, from the fifth century on, when the Church spread out into the barbarian world, it forgot to adopt the language of the people: only the educated élite could still understand the words of the liturgy. This situation lasted right up until Vatican II in the Roman Catholic Church. However, throughout those fifteen centuries people were still able to listen to the sermon and to music.

Today, like our ancestors in the early Church, we have the opportunity to celebrate in our own language. This opportunity poses considerable problems to us.

1. Many Christians, and above all many priests, have lived too long under the régime of Latin to be able to rediscover the basic essentials of listening. They have kept the habit of reading in a missal and forget that it is necessary to speak; they recite prayers and forget to pray. That is why, in our liturgies, so many of the words are nothing but droning and fine sounds; that is why our celebrations are weighed down by words which are not – spoken!

2. Under the régime of Latin, the words had another status; the sacred muttering served as a backcloth to our own individual prayer, and no attention was called for by the meaning of the words.

We might consider whether the transition to the vernacular has not necessitated a less weighty way of speaking. Paradoxically, one could put, up with a long discourse in Latin because it was unnecessary to understand it. Nowadays, because we are able to understand and therefore want to understand, are there not just too many words?

3. The evolution of communication in the modern world, strongly marked by the mass media, complicates the situation still further. We rarely have the occasion to listen to a speech together. Most of the time we are in small groups and even more often almost alone in front of a television set. We are witnessing the phenomenon of the privatization of the word; I am alone in front of my screen, and Reagan or Thatcher are speaking to me directly. Hence my desire to understand everything and make it part of me. When I go to church I would really like to

find the same listening conditions, though I am unaware of the fact. But because the liturgy is always public, is this in fact possible?

Listening in the liturgy therefore reveals plenty of traps.

'God was in the gentle breeze'

Jesus advised us, when praying, to 'go into our room and bolt the door' (Matt. 6.6). That is not a liturgical situation, and yet, in a community, prayer must not be sparing with silence.

It is impossible to find God amidst constant chatter and noise and movement. So that you can hear inside you the resonance of the spoken word, it has to stop for a moment. There is a need for silence from the lips and the body: everything stops for deep spiritual breathing. 'Breathing' and 'spiritual' are two words which have the same origin. The splendid passage from the Book of Kings (I Kings 19) where Elijah comes up against God is well known: 'God was not in the storm, nor in the earthquake, or in the fire, but in the rustle of a gentle breeze' – or, in another translation, 'in the murmuring of a held breath'. A breath, a spirit, the Holy Spirit.

Listening to the silence

Silence is the touchstone of our worship. It can be a plain absence, a dead time, a bleak and empty time when nothing happens. Or it can be being present to God, to others and to oneself, a full silence which is as capable of being felt as sound itself. Paul Claudel has said that the best thing about music is the silence which follows it. Silence listens. There is nothing stronger or more moving than the silence of a crowd which stops to hear God pass by.

'The Spirit cries out in our hearts'

There is no recipe for achieving this silence. Clocks and watches are no good. The secret is in the way of celebrating. There is a technique for

Photo Rémy Tournus

making oneself listen, and that can be learned. But the technique is no use without the essential quality of inwardness.

When the Bible is read, no matter what the words may be, it is God who speaks, and speaks first of all to those who read it; when the priest prays it is not only his prayer, still less what is set down in the missal; it is the Spirit 'who in our hearts cries out to the Father' (Gal. 4.6). When the cantor chants a couplet or the congregation the refrain, it is again the Spirit who 'comes to the aid of our weakness'; when we perform a sacramental action, it is Christ who acts.

But it is not a question of knowing whether to speak or to keep silent, to sing or not to sing. The only question is this: when I as a priest pray, in the name of my congregation; when I as a cantor or choir member sing; when I perform a certain action, am I listening to the Spirit which speaks in me, which lives in me and which works in me? In a word, am I listening to God?

If, when I speak and sing, I am listening at the same time, then I will be heard, or rather, God will be heard. That is the real question: the rest is only a matter of formula, know-how and skill. The language teachers will teach you about what we say and do, and that is necessary. But only faith can teach us how to let the Spirit live in our words and our actions, and this learning will occupy the whole of our lives.

But the Spirit is not only in me, it is also in my brothers and sisters in the assembly. Christ is in the midst of those of us who are 'gathered in his name'. So we have to listen to one another.

Keeping silent in order to speak better

Listening to one another is first of all a technical necessity. Unless one listens, neither communication nor dialogue is possible. We may say of a friend, a doctor, a priest: he knew how to listen to me. And out of this listening the word which was needed sprang to life in him (or in me). It is a great disappointment when the other person does not really listen, thinks he has understood and then immediately, as they say, 'shoots his line'!

To engage in dialogue it is essential that one speaks the same language, uses the same code. So if I want to speak with someone else, first of all I have to listen in order to learn his language, his code. Obviously my language must differ depending on whether I am speaking with a child, a manual worker, an intellectual . . .

If I am the priest presiding at the celebration, the commentator, the reader, do I take care to listen (not only with my ears but also with my eyes, with all my senses) to the congregation to whom I'm speaking, in order to know its language? It may be a silent language, but eyes and body speak, too.

When we are training liturgical commentators, we must make sure that they do not sing (especially at the microphone) at the same time as the congregation. Not only do they drown the singing of the congregation (page 79), but in addition – and this is the point here – they are unable to listen to the congregation. We should be allowed a bit of common sense.

The cantor is a transmitter (T) who, through his actions, sends a message to the congregation, who are the recipients (R).

T ⟶ R
cantor   congregation

The message of his actions will be more or less effective depending on how bad are the conditions of communication (bad visibility, interference) or how unsuitable is the body language. He will know what is happening by the message chanted back to him by the congregation, which in turn becomes a transmitter.

T ⟶ R
R ⟵ T
cantor   congregation

In order to receive this message sent by the congregation, he obviously has to keep quiet and listen. Only then can he adjust this way of sending the message so as to extract the desired response from the congregation. This is a constant two-way activity.

People may take courses in leading the assembly for centuries and never do any good unless they make this effort to listen to the congregation. On the other hand, provided that they have a good grounding, they will make rapid progress if they do listen, because they themselves will find the necessary actions and attitudes. What more can I say? Their own assemblies will make them successful.

One could say the same of the reader or the president of the assembly. Even if a congregation is silent during a sermon or reading, the person speaking will be able to hear them. He or she will note whether the silence is full or empty, whether it indicates interest or boredom. Learning to speak in public means learning to keep quiet – in order to listen.

Scoring goals

It is necessary to some degree to be aware of the physical distance covered by one's voice. Just like the footballer who, when making a pass, follows the trajectory of the ball and checks whether it has been placed rightly for his team-mate. The trajectory of the word is more compli-cated: it varies according to the instrument which utters it, the acoustics of the place in which it is projected, the means used to carry it – whether there is a microphone or not – and the congregation towards which it is directed. All these things vary, and the speaker has to reas-sess them each time. Otherwise there is a risk that the word will never reach its goal.

Photo Rémy Tournus

God is dead!

God is dead . . . when the priest, praying to God, looks at the congregation as if to persuade them that he is.

God is dead . . . when soloist's, or the choir, sing words to God and make music without being involved in what they are singing.

God is dead . . . when the reader reads from the Bible as if it were a telephone directory, without pausing for breath and without allow-ing the Spirit to breathe.

God is dead . . . when the assembly recites the Lord's Prayer or sings a hymn as if it were a popular song.

God is dead . . . when hymns no longer know how to speak to God and only aim to question with a new moralism.

God is dead . . . when the priest raises his arms to shoulder height in a mechanical gesture, no longer towards a symbolic otherness, or holds out his hands over the offerings in a mechanical gesture, and not under the weight of the Spirit.

God is dead . . . when people speak of God, carp at God, always refer to him as 'he' and not 'you'.

God is dead . . . when the word of God is not in the words, the ineffability of God is not in the silences, the Spirit is not in the bodies.

No, God is not dead, but appearances – and liturgy is all about appearances – are sometimes able to make us doubt his presence.

How to use the microphone

1. General
8 to 10 inches

2. Average
6 to 8 inches

3. Close
2 to 4 inches

Use

1. Proclamation
2. Teaching, story
3. Intimacy

1. Neutral
2. Vivacious, familiar
3. A way of giving necessary instructions so as not to disturb the atmosphere

Technique

1. Speaking as if there were no microphone
2. Speaking as though to a group six to ten feet away
3. Speaking as though taking someone into one's confidence

1. Higher tone of voice
2. Natural
3. Articulate more carefully and speak more slowly

NB: Choose your level depending on the type of remark, what you are saying, and the atmosphere. Don't overdo the intimate approach. (It can be very sensuous!)

A Church which listens

Our age suffers from a lack of inwardness. We totter under an avalanche of information, we overflow with activities, we no longer have the time to stand still. Each one of us complains about it: our development as men and women is threatened. The same goes for our faith, which is not able to blossom without this feeling of inner quiet. Isn't that what worshippers complain about when they say to us, 'There isn't enough silence at Mass!' Behind this complaint lies not so much an excess of hymns or words as a need for inner quiet. If only the Church could be above all a listening Church!

What are words good for?

You could say that words are good for speaking. However, this is one of the most complex human activities, and as it has an important place in the liturgy, it is interesting to recall the various functions words serve.

1. Contact. One example is the greeting 'The Lord be with you' – 'Hey, you there!' – 'Almighty God who . . .'
2. Information. Saying something to someone, announcing the good news.
3. Formulation. When we say to God, 'Almighty God, Merciful Father, Holy Father, Lord God

→

Almighty', we are formulating a conception of God as much to communicate this to others as to influence ourselves.

4. Expression. We express feelings of joy, grief, admiration, praise, repentance and so on.

5. Aesthetics. We like to play with our language, to juggle with it, to make poetry out of it. This is very close to symbolism. We do not content ourselves with platitudes when telling someone of our love: we compose a poem, offer a compliment, sing a song.

6. Making an impression. We invite, persuade, exhort, entreat, threaten, encourage.

7. Performative function. We have already met this word (page 13). The word which directly formulates the action that it signifies is a word which is an action. A contract made by a solicitor, mutual consent given and received, oaths, are performative words.

It is rare for a word to have only one of these aims. For example, when I address someone (making contact) I may also reveal my feelings towards him or her (expression): 'My darling', or 'Hey, you' and my words may also contain an exhortation (to make an impact): 'You there' (the implication being 'Get lost!').

In the same way, 'Almighty God, you perform wonders, blessed be your name' is a cry of admiration and praise (the phrase has an expressive function) but also a formulation: 'Almighty (i.e. God), wonders . . .'.

In fact speech consists not only of words but also of tone, rhythm, quality of voice, intensity (all musical aspects), the physical relationship between those talking, gestures and attitudes, etc.

We cannot go into detail here about the richness of the linguistic process; but let us just note that all these functions are present in the liturgy in various degrees of complexity.

The Book, books and papers

Christianity is not a religion of the Book. However, I cannot emphasize too much the respect with which the Book of the Word should be handled, a symbol which we have rediscovered and which is as important as the bread and the wine.

We can say without exaggeration that the Bible is the only book in Christian worship. Even the missal is secondary to it, although it is important because it contains the prayers of the Church.

Today, however, we have the cult of paperwork and priests are not the least offenders. Just as the Book should be handled with a degree of solemnity, so other books and papers should be handled with discretion. We can take a lesson here from the mass-media experts: do we see television presenters fiddling with sheets of paper? When all is said and done, if we have not managed to find the right page, would it not be better to change the text or pray from memory?

I might add here that the custom of giving the congregation the texts of the refrains is not perhaps the best one. Certainly on the positive side it makes it easier for them to meditate on the texts (if the texts are worth it) as well as singing them. But experience proves that when a congregation does not have the text under its eyes, provided that conditions of communication are good (of course this is very exacting for the singers) its interest is stimulated. People have to listen. They are not following a pre-programmed text. They are receptive to the word which comes to them. If we deplore an excess of words in our liturgies, ought we not also to deplore an excess of paper? We could also include in this the missal used by worshippers. Isn't it basically a tool – a very precious one – to be used in personal preparation or personal extension of the celebration? Or should it be a kind of opera score to be followed assiduously and to the letter, as sometimes actually happens with some lay people? In short, paper is only a method of communication. Let's do away with it when it isn't necessary!

16

Actions and Postures

If liturgy is all word, one could just as well say that it is all action. Our consideration of symbolic action has already shown us that.

But it would undoubtedly be useful to take a longer and more detailed look and consider the various bodily attitudes. We shall leave aside actions peculiar to specific sacraments and look at those when the time comes. Here we shall keep to those actions which are found in all liturgies.

They are symbolic actions; one cannot explain them. The person who has never made a real bow, with a movement of the whole vertebral column from the back of the head to the small of the back, will never understand its meaning. So we can only put these actions alongside other realities and raise several questions about how they are put to use.

Postures

The sitting position. 'Mary, seated at the feet of the Lord, listened to his word.' This is a fundamental attitude of listening and all that goes with it, meditation or meditative prayer. It must not be forgotten that in a long-drawn-out liturgy sitting is also a sometimes necessary attitude of rest.

The standing position. One stands for welcoming and greeting, for acclaiming or honouring (the Gospel, for example). This posture of upright man is also the symbol of the dignity of man. For us Christians it also evokes the Risen Christ, who arose in the light of Easter morning.

From a standing position we are ready to march, as the Hebrews did at the time of the first Passover.

But there are lots of ways of standing upright . . . People in the bus queue do it too. Is it the same attitude?

Walking, going from one place to another is often utilitarian, but it is often a deeply symbolic action. For obvious pastoral reasons, we are hardly ever able any longer to process from one church to another or from a chapel to a wayside cross. Processions all too often seem to be limited to marches in demonstrations. Processing is not a spectacle but an act of prayer which evokes encounter (the communion procession) and also reminds us that we are a people on the move.

Kneeling, bowing, prostrating oneself. Since the liturgical reformation began, kneeling has given way to a standing position. It must be said that it was often made into a caricature of kneeling by the prie-Dieus which we had, devices which served at the same time as an elbow rest and flap on which to put one's handbag, which with the chair made a kind of enclosure for individual religion.

Nowadays bowing is preferred, but I recognize that worshippers still rarely dare risk such a deep and expressive gesture . . .

It would nevertheless be a pity to give up kneeling completely. In times past, it was done only on fast days. It would be a good thing to reintroduce it today for rites of a markedly penitential character: for example when singing a long litany of penitence or Psalm 50, everyone, including the priest, might fall to their knees. (Genuflection, which is an act of homage, a kind of short kneeling, has also tended to give way to bowing, which it supplanted in the Middle Ages.)

As for prostration, the deepest act of humility, one does not come across it except on certain great occasions such as ordination or religious profession.

Manual actions

The action of putting one's hands together is characteristic of prayer and mental repose. It is also found in Eastern religions.

Praying with hands outstretched and open is now often preferred, as it is more biblical, older and perhaps more expressive. The open hands are symbolic of prayer as an exchange in which there is both giving and receiving, asking and thanking. Stretching out the hands is not an action limited to the priesthood and it is a good thing, for example, that the Our Father is said in this position by more and more worshippers.

The sign of the cross, the sign of death and victory, also recalls the mysterious letter T (*tau* in Greek) with which Ezekiel said that the fore-heads of worshippers were marked.

The oldest way of making the sign is only found before the gospel; the form in which it is most familiar to us is one of the first actions we learn when we are young in the faith.

It is a good thing that Vatican II reduced to four the number of times one makes the sign of the cross during the eucharist: at the beginning, at the Gospel, at the priest's epiclesis and at the blessing and dismissal. That is all the more reason for attaching weighty significance to the action.

The imposition of hands is not an action of the assembly, but a priestly action at the heart of all the sacraments (except for marriage, where it is less distinct). It is the oldest action and the richest one for blessing, calling on the Spirit and consecrating a ministry. One often finds it in the Old Testament and in the New, where by itself it

Photo Rémy Tournus

often denotes a sacrament.

Other actions still need to be mentioned:

Incensing, which is used lavishly in Eastern liturgies, symbolizes both homage paid and prayer rising. We have all heard and seen children holding their noses at the time of incensing, so incense has to be used with discretion; however, incensing is an expressive action which performs a necessary service in the liturgy to celebrate the book or an image of Christ or the assembly.

For example, in a liturgy the intention of which is to emphasize the different modes of Christ's presence, the book is censed, then, after the consecration, the bread and consecrated wine, and then, at the dismissal, the congregation.

Kissing (the Book, the altar, a picture of Christ) is also very much bound up with feelings and some people are uncomfortable about it. In daily life one does not kiss objects very much, or at least one does so in secret. In certain cultures this action can even be obscene. That is why freedom to decide has been left to conferences of bishops.

For the same reasons, the kiss of peace should often be replaced by another friendly gesture (see page 136).

Setting actions free

There are plenty of other actions: eating, drinking, singing (to which we shall return) and so on.

There are also plenty of actions which need, not to be reinvented (nothing is invented in this sphere) but to be reutilized: raising the hands for an acclamation, touching the cross to venerate it, lighting a candle in front of an icon, holding a candle at the Eastertide alleluia, and so on.

Actions are essential to our faith. Was it not by 'sending kisses to Jesus' or acting out 'in the name of the Father' that when we were very young we entered into a relationship with the invisible?

All this is a matter of the climate of worship and learning. It is important to realize that in inviting the worshippers to perform actions one is touching on profound matters which cannot be manipulated lightly. If a significant minority of worshippers still take communion in the mouth, there is no doubt that this is not just ideology; their attitude comes from something deep down inside themselves and they do not know how to explain it.

And it is important to realize that for someone who has never prayed with open hands it will be difficult, and when he or she does it first, it will seem silly. Time is needed to accustom oneself to a symbolic action, to make it one's own. Time, and patience. And also a good example from priests and those leading services.

And let us lose no opportunity of giving Christian people their freedom of initiative (see pages 38f.).

17

Landmarks to the Sacred and the Beautiful

Before looking at liturgical places, music, objects and vestments, we must pause over the dimension of the sacred and the aesthetic. These are complicated questions, a permanent source of misunderstanding and a veritable battleground. So we must content ourselves with a few landmarks.

The sacred

The sacred in paganism

Nothing is further from the gospel than a natural or pagan conception of the sacred: the sacred which sets aside things, places, times, objects and people, as the object of a tabu (don't touch!),

the rest of the universe being secular and thus escaping religion; a sacred which through its rituals claims to control the power of the deity (with magic rites, idolatry, etc.).

In this sense and only in this sense one can say that:

– There are no sacred places. The new Temple is the body of the Risen Christ, humanity made new. It is all the universe reconciled by him: 'The Mass of the world'.

– There is no sacred language. Latin has conveyed the thoughts of St Augustine and the insanities of the *Satyricon*. Besides, as St Paul said, 'let every tongue proclaim that Jesus is Lord'.

– There are no sacred instruments. For a long time the organ was forbidden because it was used to accompany lascivious dances in the 'night clubs' of the time.

– There is no sacred music. Bach uses the same language for celebrating the resurrection of Christ and celebrating coffee.

– There are no sacred objects. Everything that we use in the liturgy was originally used in everyday life – including the cross, a horrible but common instrument of torture.

These remarks are no reason for giving in to the recent trend of desacralization. For Christians precisely the opposite is true: everything is capable of being sanctified because all mankind and the whole universe belongs to Christ (read again Eph. 1.10 and Col. 1.16–20). And again: 'Whatever you eat or drink, and whatever you do, do all for the glory of God.'

The sacred in Christianity

It is tempting to banish the word 'sacred' (and its companion 'holy') from the Christian vocabulary. Yet we keep them. For several reasons (see the box on page 67), one of which has to do with human nature: an educational reason.

Let's take an example from outside religion. Their wedding ring is sacred to a husband and wife, even if they have not had a religious ceremony. And the idea of using this ring for something trivial would not occur to them. At the same time they would readily say that their love was sacred. Why do they have this respect for an object, a ring, unless it signifies a greater and sacred reality, their love?

Similarly, for Christians, sacredness does not lie in things but in the person of Jesus Christ, God's sacrament. What is sacred is their faith in God and all that that entails: their way of life, their attitude to people and the world. But the things, the places, the times are what they use to celebrate it: these themselves become objects worthy of particular respect. Just as a husband or wife would not use a wedding ring to hold up a curtain, so one would not use the eucharistic cup for a drink among friends.

For the same reason, one would not throw into the dustbin an object which had been used in worship, even though it was unsightly, damaged and useless. And a lot of tact is needed, for example, to get rid of certain statues in our churches.

There are mysteries. . . and mysteries

The word mystery can have three meanings. The first two are interconnected.

1. The biblical meaning of 'a divine plan'.

2. The liturgical sense of 'sacrament' ('mystery' is the word used for 'sacrament' in the East).

3. Finally, the word 'mystery' denotes something that cannot be explained, that goes beyond us, that reason cannot understand.

Certainly the first and second meanings have an element of the inexpressible about them, but this never goes as far as the esoteric. For us Christians the inexplicable lies in what is signified and not in what signifies, in the mystery that we are symboliz-ing and not in the forms or the language.

When Latin gave way to the vernacular, one often heard people deploring the loss of a sense of 'mystery' (in the third sense). Now not only is this idea completely foreign to the spirit of the Christian liturgy, but it is supported by historical facts: Latin specifically supplanted Greek when the latter could no longer be understood except by the élite, much to the disadvantage of the common people! From the ninth century, Latin, in its turn, was no longer understood by the people, and the Church has waited eleven centuries . . . but that is another story.

The four levels of the sacred in Christianity

1. The sacred in more or less substantial form: the body of Christ (physical body, eucharistic body, the body of the Church).

2. The sacred in sacramental form: the sacraments and the situations that they create.

3. The group of signs which express the religious relationship that we have with God in Jesus Christ. A 'pedagogical' sacredness which is purely functional is not to be confused with the sanctity of the living God.

4. All things and the whole of ordinary life which is sanctified by the use to which one puts it.

The sacred reified: or a matter of vocabulary

Christianity has not always resisted the temptation of a pagan sacredness. Many objects were the subject of tabus: a lay person might not touch a chalice, and so on.

Moreover, many rites were reified and the gap between them and objects in daily use became so wide that they seemed to belong to a sacred universe, cut off from real life. The altar bread, the host, is a good example.

The vocabulary itself is significant. The words (from a Latinized English) denoting objects are strange to us. It would be better to return to a true English vocabulary.

Host = bread
Chalice = cup
Paten = plate

Collect = opening prayer
Epistle = letter
Cruet = jugs or pitchers
Lectionary = book of the word, and so on

Of course there are things which do not have a common name, those which are not in everyday use: baptistery, eucharist or altar, for example.

This polishing up of the language would draw our attention to what these things are for: bread for eating, a plate for serving the bread on, etc. They would also help us in choosing the most suitable and the most significant forms. One question is: Doesn't the ciborium (from *cibus* = food) used for holding the altar breads resemble a chalice? That's odd!

How does the sacred manifest itself? Let us go back to our comparison with the wedding. Lots of people wear other rings and all kinds of bracelets. A wedding ring is different from the others. In what? An inscription? A special shape? A design engraved on it, as on a signet ring? Nothing like that. On the contrary, it is very plain. And it is this very plainness which gives it its meaningful difference.

Similarly, the objects which we use in the liturgy have a commonplace origin: bread, wine, music, words and so on are all things which relate to ordinary people.

So how can we indicate the distance between the commonplace and the everyday? Not necessarily – in fact not at all – by special shapes, nor by sticking crosses artificially all over the place (the cover of the ciborium with a cross for a handle, the keys of the tabernacle in the form of a cross, crosses piously embroidered everywhere, from the stole to the lace of altar cloths. I even know of a religious house where the ventilators in the skirting boards are in the form of a cross!)

The distance is mainly shown by the way in which things are used in a rite. A worshipper will not choose the music he or she has heard at the heart of the rite to relax with. The sacred is within those who make use of the objects, not in the objects themselves.

It is also shown by the quality of what is used, its 'dignity', to use a classical word from the liturgical tradition. It follows that an object or place which emphasizes the symbolization of what is all-important to us, namely the Holy God, must be full of beauty.

And that brings us to the second question, that of aesthetics.

The beautiful

There are many accepted ideas in circulation on the subject of the beautiful in the liturgy, among others the celebrated 'prayer in an ambience of beauty', which is so hackneyed and the source of so much confusion.

When in the privacy of my study I put a Bach cantata on my record player, I may be 'meditating on beauty', but I am not performing a liturgy. Bach's B Minor Mass or Beethoven's Missa Solemnis, those monuments of religious art, are not suitable for Christian worship. The most beautiful of Gothic cathedrals may turn out to be a poor vehicle for today's liturgy.

Concert performances of Masses in museum churches – does the 'Do this in remembrance of me' lie in these? At the risk of shocking some people, and mindful that the Church has played this role, we must have the courage to say that it is not the Church's vocation to be the 'patron of the arts'. The liturgy is neither the conservation of the past nor an experimental centre for contemporary music and painting, nor a hit parade of the year's successes.

After these apparently iconoclastic remarks, however, I have to stress that art and liturgy go well together. As I have already suggested, the

I think that what put me off the Church after childhood was its ugliness. Is that a frivolous, 'artistic' distaste? But what one sees counts. And the so-called City of God had a hideous decor. The clergy, those hermaphrodites in black, those temples of shadow and crouching, that old-womanly sacristy linen, that incomprehensible Latin muttered amidst the clouds of incense, communions with eyes shut and tongue outstretched with a tablemat bib, all this seemed to me irrevocably dirty – a lie, of course, but above all dirty, like the statues in Saint-Sulpice, like the morality of genuflection which the Church was teaching at that time.

That old Church was an enemy of life, the whore of the powerful and the rich! What was there about it which shocked me? If I set it down you may laugh – the sense of the sacred. For even when the sacred had not been formulated in my mind, I had an inkling of its true nature: it does not consist, as is often thought, of detaching something from reality to elevate it to some ideal but in discovering the eternal dimension in the real. So the Church seemed secular to me, though it spoke only of heaven. I sought the sacred elsewhere, below, at ground level; on faces, hands, in a word, a cry. But never in those rites cut off from all that surrounded me, uprooted from their *raison d'être* and as derisory as the traditions of the theatre – below, an earth and people; and above, this vain representation.

Morvan Lebesque, *Le Canard Enchaîné*, 4 February 1970

artist is a person familiar with symbols capable of expressing the invisible and the inexpressible. That is why artists have always quite naturally felt pretty much at home in churches, even if they do not always share our faith. The church has always appealed to them, and happily continues to do so. It is also in its way to be open to the people of its own time: Le Corbusier at Ronchamp is a good example of that.

On a recent visit to the church at Plateau d'Assy I noticed how in the tapestry of the Apocalypse which covers the back of the choir Jean Lurçat had chosen to put nothing at the centre so that the cross, placed beneath it, is brought out. This is remarkable sensitivity from an artist whose Marxist opinions are well-known, and who could not have been said to be a 'religious' artist.

Like a beautiful tool

The essential landmark in aesthetic questions is still ritual. The prime condition which a piece of music, a piece of architecture, a painting or a text must fulfil in order to be liturgical is that it

Photo F. Boissonnet

must perform a service for ritual.

We are full of admiration for the tools of ancient workmen. We put them in museums or decorate the walls of our holiday homes with them. And with good reason. The tools are beautiful because they were adapted to the hand of the person who used them.

The opposite of beauty is not ugliness but shapelessness. It is by searching out the best possible form in which to serve the ritual that the architect, the poet or the musician has the best chance of making the most beautiful shape. Find the most suitable form, and beauty will come as a bonus.

That can be just as true for the most complex tool of worship as it is for the most simple: a long litany or a short refrain, an architectural construction or a plain vase, a cathedral or a chapel.

Not the work but the action

A second landmark which follows from the first is that in this context art is not a matter of work, but of action. Even stretching things to the limit, a piece of liturgical music or a poem or a vase has no existence outside the liturgy. The misunderstanding stems from the fact that the artist wants to make a work, his own work, when, while remaining himself, he should go outside himself and enter into the perspective of the liturgical act. The musician does not compose a song to express himself, but so that his colleagues can sing it.

Clearly what he produces will be related to the quality of the action to be performed. But the way in which the song is integrated into the rite and taken over by the celebrants will be just as important as the work, if not more so.

The flowers of the field and florists' bouquets

Yes, the action is more important than the work if it is performed authentically. If your four-year-old rascal brings you a bunch of wild flowers all higgeldy-piggeldy, you are delighted. If on your birthday a grown-up gives you a bouquet which is untidy and drooping, you will at least think 'That's not up to much.'

In liturgy one cannot talk about aesthetics without also thinking about the idea of truth. There is no hesitation in choosing between an experienced organist who plays any old thing and a beginner who plays something simple, but from the heart and mindful of the needs of the service, or between a parish which employs a top florist and one in which the ladies bring flowers from their gardens. But that is not to say that the latter should not strive to improve their skills. That is also a matter of authenticity.

18

Where the Assembly Meets

'God does not live in temples made by the hands of men', said St Paul to the Athenians (Acts 17.24). The New Temple is the body of the Risen Christ where worship is offered 'in spirit and in truth' (cf. Jesus to the Samaritan woman, John 4.22f.). Christ is present 'where two or three are gathered together in (his) name' (Matt. 18.20).

So there is no longer any sacred or holy place in the pagan sense, or even in the sense found in the Old Testament. If we can say that the church is a sacred or holy place, it is only in regard to the assembly which meets there: 'a holy nation', as I Peter says.

Besides, Acts tells us that the Christians in Jerusalem continued to 'go dutifully to the temple', undoubtedly to pray there but above all

because it was a place where evangelization was possible; but when it came to the celebration unique to the disciples of Christ, 'they broke bread in their own homes' (Acts 4.42) – a marvellous freedom.

The house of God, the house of the people . . . of God

When a church is being built, the procedures are the direct opposite of pagan procedures. It is not a matter of marking out a sacred and tabu perimeter within which to enclose the deity. It is an extremely simple, extremely human matter of constructing a place to meet and worship. That is how a church comes into being. The building has to be adapted to what is to be done there, and it is an expression of the mystery of God and his people. As an instrument of worship, it has to be adapted to the assembly or assemblies which meet there and to the forms of worship which take place, and not vice versa.

The place where the assembly meets

If the assembly is the prime symbol, the place in which it meets is the first thing to look at. Liturgical teams should be reminded that before they reflect on the way in which the celebration is to be performed, it is worth looking at the space in which people meet.

To quote from the GIRM:

> 257. The people of God assembled at Mass reflects an organic and hierarchical arrangement, expressed by the various ministries and actions for each part of the celebration. The general plan of the building should suggest in some way the image of the congregation. It should also allow the most advantageous arrangement of everything necessary for the celebration and help the carrying out of each function.
>
> 273. The places for the faithful should be arranged so that the people may take full part in the celebration by seeing and by understanding everything. It is usually desirable that there be seats or benches for this purpose, but the custom of reserving seats for private persons is reprobated. Seats and benches should be arranged so that the faithful can easily take the positions required during various celebrations and so that they can readily go to communion.
>
> The faithful must be able not only to see the priest and the other ministers but also, with the aid of amplification equipment, to hear them without difficulty.

The church is primarily the place of the Church, the *ecclesia*, and the fact that the building has taken the name of what it contains is significant.

The church is first and foremost the people's house, and it was because of their awareness of this that people of early times who met in this place not only worshipped but also carried on various activities of the community (a practice which is found again today in many modern churches). The people who gather there are not satisfied just with celebrating, but they evangelize, catechize and carry out acts of charity. So the church also becomes a symbol of the Church in all its dimensions.

As the house of the people of God it is conjointly and indissolubly the house of God, for the reason that I have already given.

As in your house . . .

What you appreciate above all in your own home is its practical aspect, the way in which it is organized into spaces which reflect the various aspects of your life: eating, working, relaxing, sleeping and so on. There is usually a place for each kind of activity.

When you go into a building, you can tell at a glance what goes on there: an administrative office is quite different from a house where people live.

But at the same time the fittings, the style and the decor of a house or flat say something about the person or family who live there. In other words, if you see where someone lives, you understand something of his or her own self and personality.

Places where a rite is performed

And so, in our churches, there is a place for each rite. Presiding: 'The celebrant's chair should express his office of presiding over the assembly and of directing prayer' (GIRM 271). It is neither a throne nor a tribunal, but a place which demands that whoever performs this service faces the people (preside comes from the Latin *praesedere* = to sit in front of). In a large gathering

Photo Rémy Tournus

73

the priest will often have to be at the far end of the apse, but in a small group he will be able to position himself at the centre of a semicircle of the participants.

The 'two tables'

1. The table of the word, the lectern.
2. The altar, the place of sacrifice and the table where the meal is spread, is the centre 'which immediately attracts the attention of the faithful' even when Mass is not being celebrated, a permanent (and therefore fixed) reminder that the eucharist is the most important, the overriding purpose of every assembly. In principle there is only one altar, just as there is only one Lord and one Church. Some means must therefore be found for ensuring that side altars that one cannot remove for various financial or artistic reasons are truly of secondary importance.

Is the altar really the table for the eucharistic meal, or is it a sideboard which contains, all hurled together, the missal, the notes for the homily, the microphone, perhaps the cruets with wine and water, the purificator, the notices for the week and the priest's glasses? If our dinner tables were cluttered up like this when we had a party, what would the guests think?

There are some extensions to the altar: the credence table (this is exactly what we would call a sideboard) and the offertory table (if the collection is brought up, or even offerings in kind).

The baptistery

The Reserved Sacrament or tabernacle will preferably be in a place in the church which is conducive to prayer and adoration (and not on the altar where the eucharist is celebrated). It is a good thing to place a Bible there for worshippers to make use of. Again, the two 'tables'!

Finally, it is a good thing if there are other places in a church set aside for devotion to the Virgin Mary or some local saint.

A good link

Situations are so varied and churches so different that here I can do no more than recall the functions of each space.

But one further principle must be added, that of the relation between the various places:

It is not enough for each function to be represented by an object (altar, chair, etc.); each one needs to have an appropriate space, a space for each action.

The right link between these different spaces must be found, so that each function is presented according to its hierarchy and its distinctive character.

In short, in praying, there is a need to look for space, volume, lighting and colours and to link the different elements in a homogeneous and structured way.

Finally, it goes without saying that this whole description relates to a church with a large congregation. When a small group has a celebration it can be more flexible: at the very least particular attention should be paid to the spacing of the two tables.

The church, symbol of the Church

A rite does exist for 'dedicating', consecrating the church building. It is fairly complicated and too rarely used for us to need to spend much time on it here. I mention it because it is a development of all that is symbolic in the Church.

It is worth while reading the texts of the Mass for the dedication of churches, sometimes celebrated during the year in honour of certain great Roman basilicas (the Lateran, 9 November, and so on). Read and meditate in particular on the preface, or if you have a copy of the daily offices, the hymns for the offices of lauds and matins. And remember that the Feast of the Dedication of the Church is a feast of the Lord and his people – not a celebration of a building.

Difficulties over shape

It is by no means easy to have to celebrate the liturgy of Vatican II in churches designed for the old liturgy. I need only remind you what happens during Masses held in the two types of architecture shown in the sketches.

1

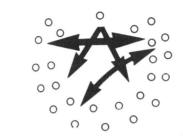

2

The arrows show the types of relationship formed

In the first plan (neo-Gothic church style) there is a forward and upward relationship, with a marked separation between the places where the principal action is carried out and an emphasis on the power of the clergy.
In the second plan there is an upward relationship which is also circular (the people can see one another); while each keeps to his or her own space, the areas of action and the 'leaders' are closer to the people.

Some styles of architecture present an almost unsurmountable obstacle, but many are capable of being modified. The whole building needs to be taken into account when modifications are to be carried out and they should be done in good taste; that calls for expert advice.

The person in your diocese responsible for religious art should be able to help you.

To give an illustration rather than a recipe, here is an example of a neo-Gothic church in which the central aisle has been done away with and the rows of seats at the side have been turned towards the choir.

It can equally be said that the place makes the assembly. So this question should occupy anyone who is concerned with the liturgy.

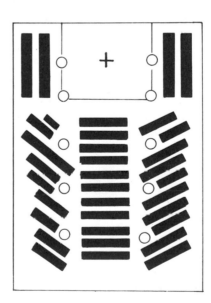

Look around your church

Go to your church. Take a new look around it.

Is the entrance area welcoming? Is it clean and attractive, or a lumber room, with old torn posters on the walls and hearse stretchers stored there?

Does it act as a transition from the street without creating a barrier between the church and the world?

Is the nave tidy, well lit, warm? How does it feel (what are the colours, the light, the smells like?)

How are the chairs arranged? Do they encourage good grouping, do they make the assembly a unit? Are they placed so that people can see one another's faces and not just backs?

Can the members of the assembly easily move and change position?

Is what goes on in the service and are the people who do things (the president, the reader, etc.) clearly visible from all sides?

Listen carefully. Are the acoustics all right? Try out the public address system: can it be heard everywhere? Is the sound well regulated, not blurred or too loud?

Look at the choir when it is lit up. What is the first thing to catch the eye?

Do the altar, the lectern and the president's chair each have their place?

Are there objects cluttering the place up to no good effect?

And so on.

19

Singing and Music

It is certainly possible to worship Jesus Christ without using music and singing. That is often done nowadays, in spite of the fact that in Christian – even biblical – tradition and by its very nature music has a privileged and structural place in the liturgy.

Perhaps you may have opened this book immediately at this chapter, because of a particular interest in the subject. If so, please go back to the chapters where I described all the riches of symbolic action. You will see that all those pages apply splendidly to making music. That is in fact one of the most basic human symbolic actions.

There is good reason why singing and liturgical music have been the object of sometimes violent quarrels throughout history. Even quite recently the abolition of Gregorian chant and the introduction of the guitar have resurrected strong feelings which still have not been entirely subdued. That is proof that singing and music are a nerve centre of Christian worship.

Music in worship

'Sacred music', 'religious music', 'church music' are all expressions in use to label works which have a connection with religion or Christianity. But for all that, such works do not fit the liturgy.

These terms are too vague: 'sacred music' might just as well denote Gregorian chant or music in the Hindu tradition: the same goes for 'religious music'. 'Church music' conjures up music performed in a church, but outside services (for example an oratorio), or music for worship. But that does not mean that it fits today's worship, because a great many works belong in a different context (e.g. Bach's B Minor Mass).

These expressions are a source of often deeply felt confusion and misunderstanding. So, like the *Universa Laus* group, I prefer terms like 'music for the Christian liturgy' or 'music for Christian worship'. For brevity, I shall speak here of 'liturgical music'.

In fact the distinguishing feature of music in worship is that it is entirely focussed on performing the service, whether the work has already been composed or a new one is being created. Thus liturgical music is first and foremost an instrument which allows communication, acclamation, meditation, proclamation, etc., all in one single act.

Music at the service of the assembly

Music is at the service of the worshipping assembly. Even if it is an art, as I have said, we have to guard against falling into the trap of art for art's sake, of idolizing the goddess music. Even if, in fact, the music performed advances the faithful in the practice of music – and they have to be helped to 'make progress' – the church is not the place for popular education. Even if, in fact, a choir derives pleasure from coming together to sing (and they ought to enjoy it, otherwise the quality will be affected), the church is not a concert hall.

The assembly comes first when music is being chosen. Whether it be music they perform or music they listen to, the music is first and foremost for the assembly, and not for the knowledgable few among them.

A difficult problem arises here, all the more so since we live in a world with very diverse cultures. In a

Photo F. Boissonnet

Photo Rémy Tournus

pluralist assembly there are very often only two ways; the middle way, which is very narrow, where common practices meet, or a mixture of styles and genres, difficult to handle without breaking the unity of the worship, but which could be a way of loving one another in diversity: a fruitful tension.

Singing

The priority of singing

In the Judaeo-Christian tradition singing has always had a privileged place over against instrumental music. The Church has not turned its back on instrumental music, but it has always

Photo Rémy Tournus

Sisters of St Paul of Kinshasa. *Photo E.P.A.*

been slightly mistrustful, because such music can sometimes lead to uncontrollable ecstasy (that may seem surprising, but one has only to think of certain practices in modern society, where music is used like a drug). Above all else, the Church has always accorded singing a privileged place because it is linked with the word, the place of which in Christian liturgy we have already discussed.

Words and music

A word of warning! A chant is not a text sprinkled with music. Two different musical settings will make the same text say different things (cf. e.g. Kyrie I with Kyrie XVII). Text and music react on one another, the latter adding a dimension that cannot be put into words. It is important to take account of the universal appeal of singing when choosing music for worship.

It is also necessary to understand the relationships between chant and music. These can be roughly grouped into three types:

1. The only function of the music is to carry the word, like a humble servant. Instances are recitative, psalmody, cantillation (e.g. a sung version of Preface or the Lord's Prayer).

2. Music and words go together. Examples of this category are hymns or well-written canticles. You cannot say which is the more important: one goes with the other.

3. The music takes wing and the words become almost a pretext, e.g. a Gregorian Alleluia with its long garlands of melody. The word alleluia naturally becomes music.

'Singing' and faith

'Tell me what you sing and I will tell you what you believe.' Because music moves words into a new dimension, because it endows them with its own characteristics, the quality of what is in the repertoire is vital for faith. To give an example: at the beginning of the century people used to sing:

I have only one soul to be saved,
    May I keep it from fire everlasting.
Wasn't this hymn both the source of a type of believing and a reflection on it?

An action

First, one all too often forgets that singing is an action: not only a vocal action but one involving the whole body.

It may be a community action, and that is why singing is so important in congregational activity, because it helps everyone to express themselves.

It may be an action performed by one person on behalf of everyone (the cantor, the deacon or the priest).

Singing is a ritual action, whether it be part of the rite (for instance the acclamation alleluia) or accompanies the rite (for example the processional hymn at the communion). At this level, if the singing is done in good conditions, one can count on the worship being well done. If I choose a good alleluia, a good acclamation, if everything works together so that it is really sung as an acclamation, the rite will have been well performed.

But at another level, that of symbolism, singing produces meaning. As we have seen, nothing can get the better of it; it delights us, hits us, overwhelms us, surprises us, revolts us, and so on.

Form and depth

A third consideration ought to be taken account of in the choice of what is sung. Take Psalm 118 on Easter Day. Sing it with a refrain before and after the verse. Then sing it, putting the refrain between each strophe. A third way is to sing it with an alleluia to punctuate each verse.

Yet a fourth way is to have a repeated alleluia sung softly and the psalms read quietly above it. In each case the text is the same, but each method is different and each one in fact says something different.

When one takes a great tropary as an opening hymn, like 'Children of the Same Father', it says just about everything and, thanks to the form, achieves everything.

So it is important to choose the form to fit the ritual situation in which music is sung. See, for example, the communion and post-communion chants (pages 140).

The repertoires

Because by its very nature worship is repetitive, the assembly as a whole needs a repertoire. First of all for the practical reason that it cannot always be learning; and in order to be able really to get into a chant one has to know it well. Then for the aesthetic reason that some pieces of music cannot reveal their full meaning unless they are well performed. And above all, each chant is an experience in itself to the degree that is used.

Any young people who have been to Taizé will relive their visit whenever they sing one of the low-toned chants again; their whole pilgrimage will come back to anyone who sings a Lourdes canticle. Listen to *Rorate caeli desuper* and the Advents of your childhood will come flooding back into your memory; listen to Kyriale I and it is Easter, and so on. That is an interesting fact to take into account when choosing chants.

These are the most common musical forms in the liturgy:
1. Response, invocation, litanies (brief interventions by the congregation)

2. Couplet refrain

3. Hymn

4. Tropary (a more complex form which integrates 1 and 2), e.g. stanza, refrain, litany, refrain, stanza, refrain.
5. Riff (a term of jazz origin: a repetitive rhythmic melodic formula on which sung or spoken material is superposed)

What should one choose? All ways are open, bearing in mind the pastoral gifts available. There is everything from the repertory of Gregorian chant to the most contemporary music, and there is no reason *a priori* to do away with this or that part of our heritage.

Although it is still evolving, the repertoire should have a degree of stability. The excess of new things which we have had over the past fifteen years cannot go on for ever. In view of the vast numbers of new chants produced (around 6,000), some discernment is necessary: it is wrong to be seduced by often deceptive performances on record or by the commercialism of certain singer-composers. And it is vital for the experts to make their judgment.

Alongside the repertoire proper (hymns, canticles, etc.) the assembly should have some 'operative models' at its disposal: a recitative for singing the psalms, a well-known tune to which one can put simple words to make a refrain to the general intercessions, a cantillation which allows for a degree of improvisation, and so on. This allows an element of freshness to be brought into the worship, a uniqueness which is complementary to the repetition. The rite is always the same, always new.

Musical instruments

Although they are not indispensable – the Eastern churches do not use them – instrumentalists perform a real service to the worshipping assembly.

They accompany the singing and thus make it easier.

They create an environment of sound for rites and 'fill in' space.

They enrich worship by performing significant works.

Sometimes, in a secondary way, they can even express the voice of the assembly.

Finally, they can bring the riches of a newer language than the assembly can use, one which signifies the radical newness of the gospel.

Listening

Don't let's forget that listening is also a form of participation. Through a concern to make the assembly sing, instruments (and choirs) have been excessively silenced. Broadly speaking one can distinguish three kinds of listening:

1. Absent-minded listening – just as a record can provide background music at a party so the organist playing before the Mass makes the church more welcoming and creates an atmosphere.

2. Indirect listening – film music is of this kind. In church this is music which accompanies a procession or forms an underlying accompaniment to words.

3. Direct listening. Here the music is the worship; this avenue has not yet sufficiently been explored. For example, at a wedding at which people do not sing, ask the organist to play a suitable piece of music after the exchange of vows.

Recorded music

Until further notice, the use of electro-mechanical means of reproduction is forbidden in worship. Why should there be such a harsh order?

It is hard to see how this rule can be observed today. But we ought not to forget its spirit: nothing can replace the action of people of flesh and blood. Beware of a press-button liturgy! That's a real danger.

Moreover, this method requires delicate handling. The technicalities must not be obvious (those scratched discs or recordings which are suddenly interrupted). Besides, it would sound wrong to put a huge organ like that of Notre Dame in Paris into a little village church; and if the organist is present, it is a slight on him.

Finally, it would be a pity if the Church were to imitate the big department stores or even our modern living conditions, where nothing can go on without piped music.

At the service of the assembly

The leader of the singing

The leader performs one part of the role traditionally played by the deacon (particularly in the East), which is to make a link between the choir and the nave.

He helps the congregation to express itself, particularly through singing. His job consists in the more humble duties, like giving a page, bringing people in at the right time, and also, if he can, helping the congregation to give of its best.

In antiphonal singing, if there is no choir he is the one who sings the couplets and verses, but is silent when it is the turn of the congregation to sing.

He has to play his part efficiently and discreetly: the main figure in the eucharist is the president. He must learn to do whatever is necessary but not more than is necessary, in other words not to interfere when there is no need. In that way his power will become more effective.

The choir

The choir is both part of the assembly and complementary to it. This double role will govern the choice of its place within the area where the celebration takes place.

Members of the choir should not forget that they are the reflection of the assembly. It is a happy parish where the people say, 'You can see the choir praying', and it is a happy choir whose members can say, 'You can see our leader praying.'

This requirement makes other technical demands (scores properly in order, a precise knowledge of the programme, good intonation in the starts, and so on) which a concert choir does not have to deal with.

The choir is at the service of the assembly, and ought to help it to express itself. That is why it has to resist the always gratifying temptation of indulging in part-singing, when the congregation is not totally familiar with the tune. The choir also has to know how to give up an item which it enjoys, if this turns out to be not in the best interests of the flow of the worship, etc.

Besides being complementary to worship, like the instruments it gives worship a new and rich meaning.

The organist

The organ does not play itself; the organist is a creature of flesh and blood, as much a believer as possible. He ought also to be closely associated with preparations for the service, at the very least knowing what is to be done well in advance down to the last detail.

He deserves respect; for example, the congregation should realize that one cannot turn off a Bach fugue as easily as a radio set. They should try to help organists to use their talents and the riches of their instruments in the service of the liturgy.

In short, one expects the qualities of any liturgical ministry from all those concerned with the music.

20

Objects and Vestments

Objects

Ritual objects

Our constant aim should be towards truth in words, truth in attitudes and actions. But that will not happen without truth in respect of the objects used in the rite. Most of them are still a legacy from the pre-Vatican II liturgy: many of them no longer have any significance or, more precisely, now mean something else. Deprived of their earlier function, they are in a form which no longer fits the present-day liturgy. Vatican II has relieved us of a great many things, like the maniple or the altar cards. That is all the more reason for treasuring those objects which we cannot do without: they must be beautiful, but above all they must signify something. The two qualities go hand in hand.

This does not require a major financial investment: it is rather a matter of good taste, vigilance, even ingenuity.

The Book should look attractive on the outside, perhaps decorated with an icon or covered with embroidered material.

The patten should be a real plate and not a saucer perched on the chalice (does one put a plate on a glass?).

The old ciboria, which to worshippers look just like chalices, do not suggest the idea of food.

As for the water and wine, little earthenware jugs can easily be found, but of a pleasing shape and more attractive than the cruet.

The aspersion should wet effectively.

The candles should be real candles, even if that

Polypytch of the Last
Supper. Detail.
Dirk Bouts. Louvain.
Photo Giraudon

means less of them.

The thurible should smoke. If it doesn't, don't use it!

What use is the sanctuary bell now? When the Mass was in Latin it acted as a signal. Today it cannot be more than an object for high days and holidays for which a new use has to be found.

The cross, whether or not it is processional, should be beautiful, with a well-proportioned shape, and it should be put in the proper place.

In short, are we as demanding over objects in worship as we are over those we use when we invite friends to our house?

And what significance do they have – not in theory but in fact? The GIRM gives considerable latitude in the choice of form and material, so we should take advantage of it.

Vestments

It may be useful to remind ourselves of the meaning of liturgical vestments. In contrast to everyday clothing they are:

1. A sign: in a group one needs to mark out someone with a special role to play.

2. A symbol: the person who wears them is more than Father X; he is the living sign of the Christ who calls us together. These two ideas should guide every adaptation and rethinking.

It is doubtful whether all the vestments would be meaningful to people today without archaeological explanations which have to be given or symbolism invented after the event (like the amice, which originally was a neck scarf, and has now become 'the helmet of salvation'). Fortunately Vatican II has lessened the panoply and research is being carried on into creating vestments which are simple and significant, corresponding better to our sensibilities (care is needed, because some suppliers have the worst cheek by jowl with the best). Cleanliness, simplicity and dignity are the three qualities of liturgical vestments which contribute to the truth of our celebration.

21

The Liturgical Year

For the Christian, there is no sacred and profane time in the strict sense because 'we do well always and everywhere to give you thanks'.

However, just as our lives are measured out by anniversaries, so it is natural to celebrate the mysteries of the Lord in a recurrent pattern. We need both Sunday and the liturgical year: they are part of 'sacred pedagogy' (see page 66).

Gabriel, aged ten, asked: 'Why do we keep Christmas and Easter in the same year? We ought to celebrate Christmas, and then Easter thirty-three years later.'

Even if Easter is the actual date of Jesus's death (more or less, as the calendar has been somewhat modified since then), for us it is never a mere anniversary but a concrete and evocative way of celebrating the Paschal mystery which we have to live out all our lives.

On the other hand, our liturgical year is a quite different experience from the seasonal cycles celebrated by the pagan cults (which we find today in the secularization of Christmas in the winter and Easter in the spring).

In pagan worship it is a closed cycle, more or less marked by fatalism and ultimately static, whereas for Christianity history has a direction; it is going somewhere, towards a goal.

pagan time

But as our existence is also marked out by the annual cycle, this pattern can be turned into a spiral, each revolution representing one year.

Christian time

Every year, we celebrate again the same mysteries (anniversaries), but as we celebrate them, in trying to live them out in our lives we are journeying towards the end of time. The history of salvation is that of a people on the march: it is a time that goes from the creation to the new creation, and this new world is being built up in the present-day life of humanity, from day to day and from year to year. We are extended between two poles: the coming of God among us and his historical Easter on the one hand, and his return at the final Easter on the other.

Sunday

A revolution

The Church of the apostles immediately set itself apart from the Jewish tradition by replacing the sabbath with the day after, the first day of the week (and not the last, as our modern customs might make us believe), as if to show that the resurrection of Christ ushered in a new time. Revolutionaries have always liked changing the calendar . . . Moreover this first day of the week, soon called 'the Lord's Day' (Rev. 1.20), a term which itself recalled the Day of Yahweh (look it up in your Bible) was full of the symbolism of the creation. With the resurrection a new world was born. It is in this sense that certain traditions also call it 'the eighth day': a new world, a new time. In addition, in the Roman world it was the 'day of the sun': one could not have a better dream.

A weekly Easter

Sunday is a weekly Easter. This is demonstrated by the evangelists' insistence on showing that

the resurrection manifests itself in the Church gathered together on the first day of the week.

It is worth noting that in the early centuries

The Lord's Day in the Bible	
'God said, "Let there be light" and there was light. There was evening, there was morning: the first day' (Gen. 1).	**First creation (light)**
'Now on the first day of the week came Mary Magdalene to the tomb early' (John 20.1)	**Resurrection**
'On the evening of that day, the first day of the week . . . Jesus came and stood among them' (John 2.19).	**Manifestation of the Risen Lord to the gathering of disciples**
'Eight days later . . . Jesus came and stood among them' (John 20.26).	
'On the first day of the week, when we were gathered together to break bread' (Acts 20.7)	**The early Church celebrates the eucharist and shows its brotherly love**
'Now concerning the contribution for the saints . . . On the first day of every week, each of you is to put something aside and store it up, as he may prosper, so that contributions need not be made when I come' (I Cor. 16.2)	
'The night is far gone, the day is at hand. Let us then cast off the works of darkness and put on the armour of light' (Rom. 13.12).	**in preparing for the day of Christ's return**

The Christian year

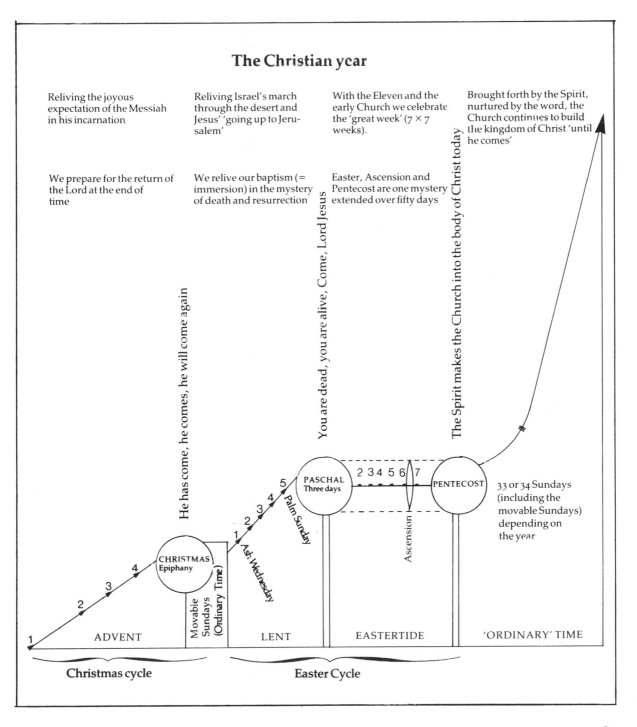

Reliving the joyous expectation of the Messiah in his incarnation

Reliving Israel's march through the desert and Jesus' 'going up to Jerusalem'

With the Eleven and the early Church we celebrate the 'great week' (7×7 weeks).

Brought forth by the Spirit, nurtured by the word, the Church continues to build the kingdom of Christ 'until he comes'

We prepare for the return of the Lord at the end of time

We relive our baptism (= immersion) in the mystery of death and resurrection

Easter, Ascension and Pentecost are one mystery extended over fifty days

He has come, he comes, he will come again

You are dead, you are alive, Come, Lord Jesus

The Spirit makes the Church into the body of Christ today

1 2 3 4

CHRISTMAS Epiphany

Movable Sundays (Ordinary Time)

Ash Wednesday

1 2 3 4 5

Palm Sunday

PASCHAL Three days

2 3 4 5 6 7

Ascension

PENTECOST

33 or 34 Sundays (including the movable Sundays) depending on the year

1 ADVENT

LENT

EASTERTIDE

'ORDINARY' TIME

Christmas cycle

Easter Cycle

Sunday was a working day and that Christians had to make an effort to meet together. They also met at night, as we see from Acts 20.7. (We find this situation again in our secularized Sunday, where it is often necessary to give up all kinds of activities in order to go to Mass; Christians living in Islamic countries know the same situation.)

So rest is not an essential element of Sunday.

The day of the eucharistic assembly

A strong link joins up the Church – the assembly – Sunday.

Sunday is not a day for 'making one's communion' in order to be right with God, but for meeting in assembly.

For a long time there was only one meeting of the local assembly on a Sunday; for symbolic reasons (the assembly is where the local Church is) and pastoral reasons (it is there that church activities converge and it is from there that they take their source).

This assembly is eucharistic by nature; even if because of a lack of priests it is unable to celebrate the sacramental eucharist, after celebrating the word it gives thanks to God.

Today?

We have already raised the question of the multiplicity of Masses. One might also question the extension of Sunday to Saturday evening. One cannot help but be glad about it for all those many Christians who are prevented from attending on Sunday for good reasons, but we must be suspicious when we hear people, even priests, suggest that Mass should be anticipated on Friday evening before people go off for the weekend. That is a more serious question than it might seem: if Sunday is extended in this way, must it not then lose its symbolism? In any case, whatever the difficulties, it is clear that the Church has always kept this original nucleus.

In former times Sunday also used to be an occasion for gatherings other than Mass (e.g. Vespers). In spite of changes in rhythm and incursions into leisure time, some parishes today are trying to restore a time for prayer.

Contemporary Christians might ask themselves whether or not they want to make Sunday into a day illuminated by the resurrection and filled with praise and joy.

———

The Paschal mystery and the liturgical year

The liturgical year has been gradually built up (see the table) out of several cycles:

1. The Paschal cycle, the original centre of which is certainly the Paschal Vigil.

It was extended by the fifty days which lead up to Pentecost (*pentecoste* means fifty), or seven weeks of seven days.

A time of preparation came into being before that, namely Lent.

At the same time the Paschal Vigil extended over three days, the Paschal triduum which in turn gave rise to Palm Sunday and Holy Week.

2. The Christmas cycle. The festival of Christmas did not come into being until the fourth century. In fact it was a way of taking over the pagan festival of the winter solstice, because there is no indication that Jesus was born on 25 December. The same goes for Epiphany (from the Greek *epiphania*, showing) in the East, where the solstice was celebrated on 6 January.

Towards the sixth century, just as there was Lent before Easter, so Advent came into being as a preparation for Christmas.

Finally, the Feast of the Presentation of Christ (Candlemass) is an extension of the Feasts of the Nativity.

The Paschal mystery is present, even at Christmas

The weekly celebration of Easter must not be lost sight of: whether it be the First Sunday in Advent or the Twenty-Seventh Sunday in Ordinary Time, we are always celebrating Christ crucified and risen. The risen Christ is the star which illuminates our whole year, and it is he who makes every facet of the mystery of our faith shine, through the sequence of Sundays and festivals.

The pastoral consequences of this are manifold. Let me illustrate it by taking as an example the popular festival of Christmas, which is unfortunately more popular than Easter. A celebration which did not 'shake off' the image of the infant Jesus would not be in line with the faith: certainly, the symbolism of Christmas is fine and good, but it will be badly misused if one does not at the same time see in it the whole destiny of God made man, which reaches its fulfilment in the paschal sacrifice. Besides, if we are alert in what the liturgy has to offer us, we shall be unable to deface the mystery of Christmas, because in it we celebrate the eucharist which is the passover of Christ.

The liturgical year is a perpetual *anamnesis*, or remembering. Every festival is celebrated in three dimensions of time: yesterday, today and tomorrow. Take Christmas, for example: he came, two thousand years ago; he comes among us today (through the Church, through our conversion) and one day he will return.

Through the year

We do not have space here to look at every festival in detail. So you should look at your missal and the introductions it contains, or at other books.

Let me just stress the spirit of these festivals, on the basis of their essential rites.

1. Advent, from the Latin *adventus* (going before), in Greek *parousia*. This denoted the presentation of the divine statue to the people. The term *parousia* in Christian vocabulary denotes Christ's return at the end of time. That tells us something about the spirit of Advent, which points both towards Christ's return: 'Prepare the way of the Lord.'

A time of preparation, Advent has always been less austere than Lent. The Third Sunday even brims over with joy.

2. Christmas, Epiphany, the Baptism of Jesus. The first is more important in the West, the second in the East. But the three festivals are not too much to exploit all the riches of the mystery of God made man.

Christmas puts more stress on the human birth of Christ, on his appearance to the 'poor' (Joseph, Mary, the shepherds).

Epiphany has its emphasis more on the manifestation of Jesus to all nations (the magi) as the Son of God. It celebrates the universality of the Church.

The baptism is the manifestation of Jesus as the Son of God at the beginning of the mission which will lead him to Easter.

3. Lent was originally a time when many Christians fasted voluntarily on certain days. It also became the time when the catechumens prepared themselves for baptism and penitents for forgiveness. It then became a time of conversion and of listening to the word of God for the Church as a whole, and also a time for pondering afresh the great symbols of baptism (often evoked by the Gospel writers).

It is an important time for the Church, a kind of collective 'retreat' when it renews its baptism by associating itself with Christ's struggle. Lent lasts for forty days. Forty, in the Bible, is the time of testing (the Flood, the Hebrews, then Jesus in the wilderness), the once-in-a-lifetime opportunity when people have the chance to transform themselves.

It begins somewhat in advance with the ritual of Ash Wednesday, formerly intended for penitents who were temporarily excluded from the assembly as Adam was excluded from Paradise (hence the formula: 'Remember that you are dust'). Today this is perhaps the most beautiful of the penitential celebrations.

4. Holy Week

(a) It begins with Palm Sunday. Here again the double theme of death and resurrection is present: we begin with the triumph of the palm procession, the forerunner of Easter, continue with the celebration of the passion and end with the eucharist.

(b) The Paschal triduum: Holy Thursday, Good Friday and Holy Saturday. They form a whole, with the vigil as a climax (not the Sunday). It is necessary to be aware of this in pastoral terms and in the method of celebrating it (for example, by using recurrent items, the same cross, the same hymn, throughout the three days).

Holy Thursday (Maundy Thursday): At the centre is the institution of the eucharist, the new Passover, and its translation into action, the foot-washing (either just read, or then mimed as well).

Good Friday is a synthesis of two kinds of service, the one Western, concentrating on the passion, the other Eastern (the triumphal veneration of the cross). The old tradition of not celebrating the eucharist has been retained: com-

munion is made from the reserved sacrament.

Holy Saturday has the rites of fire and light (the symbolism of light and darkness). There is
 – a developed liturgy of the word.
 – a baptismal liturgy
 – a eucharistic liturgy
 – an agape.

(c) The fifty days of Eastertide. Now begins the great week, the week of seven weeks, which ends at Pentecost. This is the 'Great Sunday'.

It was only later that the unity of these fifty days was broken by the Feast of the Ascension, which is yet another way of celebrating the resurrection (see John 20.17).

(d) Pentecost. Harvest festival in the Old Testament. According to Luke it was the day on which the Church was born in the power of the Holy Spirit, and when it was sent into the world (according to St John all this also took place at the resurrection, see John 20.21–23).

5. Ordinary time. All the other Sundays. Given the fact that Easter is a moveable feast, a greater or lesser number of Sundays come between the Easter cycle and the Christmas cycle. The last ones are clearly centred on Christ's return. In a way they meet up with the season of Advent.

6. Festivals linked to the civil calendar. Outside the liturgical year there is what is called the sanctoral, the festivals of the saints.

These are of secondary importance compared with Sundays and with the two cycles discussed above, except for a few which can supplant an ordinary Sunday.

91

PART THREE

The Eucharistic Liturgy

We have seen that the assembly is already in itself the symbol of the divine work realized in the course of history: it brings about the meeting together of redeemed humanity. But it is through the essential Christian celebration, the eucharist, that it becomes fully sacramental: it brings about the covenant.

That is what is shown by the various rites the significance of which I shall now describe.

Names for the eucharistic celebration

Missus, sent: according to some people this term formerly marked the beginning of the eucharistic liturgy when the catechumens were sent away. Hence the word Mass, which therefore would denote the beginning of the celebration. It has ended up by being used for the whole service. This is a pity. The terms used in the New Testament were much more evocative:

– The Lord's supper (I Cor. 11.20–33).
– The breaking of bread (Luke 24.36; Acts 2.42–46)
– There is also mention of eucharist (thanksgiving) (Luke 24.30; I Cor. 11.24; Acts 27.35), a term already used in Jewish ritual.

In the second century eucharist clearly denoted the sacrament of bread and wine. The terms sacrifice and offering (*oblatio*) were also used.

In Greek, offering is *anaphora* (to lift upwards). The Eastern Church therefore calls the eucharistic prayer the anaphora. It also uses the terms synaxis (assembly, whether sacramental or not), liturgy (public worship), sometimes kyrial (the Lord's) to denote the Sunday celebration.

In the West we also had the word collect (gathering up).

The reality denoted is always the same: the assembly giving thanks through the offering of Christ.

22

Assembling

An important time of welcome

When friends come to your home for dinner, you do not immediately sit down at the table. The time when you welcome them is important, and has its rites: the arrangement of the sitting room, light, music, flowers. After the guests have been welcomed at the door, an aperitif allows them to relax and get to know one another. They find out about one another and the hostess is careful not to rush things.

The same thing happens at a liturgical gathering. There are obvious psychological reasons why we should not neglect this process if we believe that the assembly is 'the first sign' (see chapter 9). Moreover, if you understand the directions given in the missal you will soon see that this is the idea behind the rites which are suggested for the beginning of the eucharist.

'After the people have assembled, the entrance song begins' (GIRM 25). After the people have assembled! Is it a real assembly? Has it been encouraged to be an assembly beforehand?

When people arrive at church are they met by faces (the priest, a lay person handing out hymn books or giving directions . . .)?

What kind of place do they come to? Is it welcoming (see page 76)? Has the organist been asked to play background music? Does the atmosphere encourage people to keep them-

Arriving on time!

Before Vatican II people talked of the 'foremass' which amounted to a relative devaluation of everything before the Mass proper, which began at the offertory. It was enough to have arrived at this moment to have respected the Lord's command.

The consequences of this attitude linger on. How many worshippers think that the time of welcome and listening to the word is unimportant! It is a fortunate parish where people can be heard to say:

'Something happened to make me late. I feel that I missed out on something.'

The eucharistic liturgy and the liturgy of the word are 'so closely connected as to form one single act of worship', says the GIRM (8). But how can one enter fully into the liturgy of the word if one has missed the time of welcome, which establishes the community?

---

selves to themselves or, on the other hand, to turn to their neighbours with a smile or even a quiet word, without disturbing the recollection necessary for Christian celebration . . .

If there is a rehearsal for worship does the commentator say good morning, as one would do at any gathering, or does he just launch in with 'Turn to page 147'? Is the rehearsal already a way of entering into fellowship or just a laborious singing lesson?

The entrance song (or better, the opening song) is something of an aperitif (from the Latin *aperio* = open). It is the most normal and most immediate way of doing something together: it opens people's mouths, opens their hearts, gets them to move their bodies – and the body is the most important and indispensable instrument of

worship (see pages 11, 79). That is the first aim of the entrance song: 'to open the celebration and deepen the unity of the people' (GIRM 25). Experience proves that the song chosen should be a well known one, or at least one which is easy to sing.

At the same time the function of this song is to 'introduce the people to the mystery of the season or feast' (GIRM ibid.), by its content or by the liturgical use to which it is put (for example, if certain songs are kept for Advent, they will act as a signal). But if there is any contradiction between these two functions of bringing the people together and introducing the mystery of the day, then there should be no hesitation in preferring the first, which is of prime importance for the worship which follows.

After the chant, 'the priest and congregation make the sign of the cross'. This is a second symbolic gesture, a password among Christians who recognize one another by this sign of the Trinity. Again it is important that this symbol does not degenerate into a signal. In many other contexts, for example at grace before meals, 'In the name of the Father' is a signal for a pause and for recollection: 'Let's be serious for a moment, keep quiet, it's beginning.' In order to give full meaning to this gesture it will be enough to modify slightly the way in which it is made

The ritual pattern

Entrance chant
Sign of the cross, greeting, welcome
Penitential act
Gloria
Opening prayer

AMEN

(re-read page 19), e.g. by introducing it with the words 'Let us sign ourselves with the sign of our faith' or occasionally, making it slowly and in silence, or even omitting the gesture altogether.

'Then through a greeting the priest expresses the presence of the Lord to the assembled community' (GIRM 28). As we have seen (page 42), the Christian community is an organic body. This is what the opening dialogue symbolizes. In a dialogue there are two participants: here the assembly and, in front of them, the one who in its midst has the ministry of being the sign of God who calls his people together.

The priest can use as an example one of the three more or less developed formulae given in the missal.

'After greeting the people, the priest or other suitable minister may very briefly introduce the Mass of the day' (GIRM 29). What is an introduction, unless it is to allow the assembly to pass from the everyday to celebration, 'from the street to the Amen', to use a phrase of Gelineau's? This is exactly what the hostess does (page 48). It is the ministry of the priest to make the link . . . But in certain cases it can be very meaningful and significant for the people of God if a lay person undertakes the task.

Then comes the penitential preparation. It is presented by the priest as he wills, and can follow several forms. This rite, and particularly the importance that it has assumed in the practice of our parishes, deserves some thought.

One may note that the rite is often inflated. Is it not significant that in many places it is sung, and the Gloria is recited? Even worse, its content is often one of imputing guilt (even some missals fall into this error).

That seems to go against common sense.

First of all it goes against psychological common sense. People arrive, they are happy to be together in the Lord, and then all of a sudden someone flings death, judgment, heaven and hell at them. We are put in mind of the famous comment of Péguy who reproached Christians for spending the time on the doorstep 'wiping their feet'. It is for this reason that the marriage service provides for the possibility of lightening the opening and omitting this rite (which does not mean, though, that we do not recognize that we are sinners).

It also goes against common sense in gospel terms. We are not converted by blaming ourselves, nor by our remorse at having failed to live up to the ideal image of ourselves. What reconciles us is the word of God, listening to and contemplating the God of love. It is the word of God which shows me my sin, and it is here that we can recognize the fundamental process of the sacrament of reconciliation.

So what we are doing here is not so much 'examining our consciences' as being generally aware of our situation in respect of a God who loves us, who is the Holy One, the Wholly Other, and so of our need of being saved. We are a people of redeemed sinners. This act of penitence is of great pastoral importance; it is all that, but it cannot be more than that. The most recent phrases in the missal of Paul VI put it well: 'Lord Jesus, you were sent to heal the contrite', or 'You who live with the Father and draw us towards him, may you be blessed! Have mercy on us.' Penitence is first and foremost a matter of looking towards an other, and what an Other that is!

After the penitential preparation comes the *Kyrie eleison* (unless the third formula has been followed), 'an acclamation which praises the Lord and implores his mercy' (GIRM 30). The remains of a litany now vanished which from a very early stage was used at the beginning of worship because of what was then its popular character, this Greek phrase means 'Lord (the Risen Christ) have mercy'. It might seem somewhat surprising that it comes after the absolution: does not logic suggest that it should be shifted slightly? Be this as it may, this acclamation is valuable and could be well used to punctuate the invocation of formulas 2 and 3.

The Gloria, too, is a very ancient hymn. A trinitarian hymn, it was used first of all at the festival of Christmas, then spread progressively to all feast days and finally to every Sunday outside the penitential seasons, specifically as a sign of celebration.

Hymns mean music – at least in a large assembly. Imagine the President of the French Republic or of the United States, saying, And now let us say the Marseillaise or the Star Spangled Banner! So the most usual thing is for this hymn to be sung, either by everyone together or antiphonally: however, if it is sung antiphonally the division should be between two halves of the congregation or between congregation and choir and not, as often happens, between the priest and the congregation (when it is spoken), since at this moment the priest ought to be identified with the congregation.

Then, as at the end of every major rite, comes a prayer said by the president, called the opening prayer. The priest first of all invites the people to pray and 'together they spend some moments in silence so they may realize that they are in God's presence and may make their petitions' (GIRM 32). Care should be taken over this silence: if there is no true silence one might as well leave out the invitation 'Let us pray.'

This prayer, which is still called a collect, 'expresses the theme of the celebration' (GIRM 32). I mentioned earlier the problem which besets so many actual prayers (page 47), and we do not need to go back to it. Be this as it may, the collect ought to – should have – encapsulate(d) all the dynamic of the entrance rite, gathering into one all its content and directing us towards this God who brings us together to feed us with his word and with his bread. The people make this prayer their own by responding Amen.

The aim of the entrance rite

And so, from the moment when the people come together until the final Amen, all the parts of the service, each with a different emphasis, work together to form the Lord's assembly, that is to say:

– to make us recognize that we are brothers and sisters, members of Christ;
– to show that we are one people, a single body;
– a structured, organized body;
– to set us, in Jesus Christ, before a Father who redeems us.

The opening ought also to 'introduce the Mass of the day'. How this is done varies, depending on the pastoral situation. It is possible for the opening to be made virtually 'neutral' (that is the case particularly with monastic congregations, where only the opening hymn and the collect vary).

But often, especially in Sunday worship in a parish, people will want to add colour to the unfolding of the worship by means of the theme for the day: through the chant, if possible; the welcome, the penitential section and the final prayer; it is even desirable that the decoration (flowers, pictures, posters) should convey the same theme.

One thing, however, must be guarded against. The opening is not a summary of the celebration in the way that an overture to an opera is. Heaven preserve us from such phrases as 'Soon St Paul will tell us that . . .' No, it is a matter of preparing good ground for the word of the day to be sown (the farmer does not put down any old fertilizer for any old seed). The opening is a time of awakening, of becoming aware, a time of convocation; it can also be a time of provocation!

Assemblies without a priest

The rite is not substantially different from that of the Mass, but one can profit from simplifying it to make it more effective:
– mutual welcome (including welcome of those who do not normally come)
– invitation
– chant
– collect
  It is an advantage to have the penitential rite later on, either during the liturgy of the word or in the rite of communion (before or after the Lord's Prayer). The invitation can be expressed in the following way:

The processional cross is brought in ('I am in the midst of you') and the sign of the cross is made.

Not a greeting but a benediction is said, for example: 'May God, the Father of our Lord Jesus Christ, bless us and bring us together in communion with the Holy Spirit. Amen.'

Experience

The missal is full of suggestions for the opening of worship.

But there is another side to the coin. With experience one is more or less strongly aware of the pairings: between the word of welcome and the word which introduces the act of penitence, between the silence of this last rite and that of the concluding prayer, between the sign of the cross and the trinitarian greeting, between the act of penitence and the phrases of supplication within the Gloria, and so on. Above all one gets bothered by the multitude of ritual elements in so short a time, and even more by the multiplicity of chants (at least three) that the congregation does not have time to make its own, to enjoy to the full. Scarcely has one started one course than it is replaced by another! One finds oneself missing the simplicity of the primitive liturgies which are still used on Good Friday.

A Gloria sung out loudly, a *Trisagion* (an acclamation to God consisting of 'Holy' sung three times followed by the Kyrie) will often suffice as a single hymn. In some congregations a silence, if it is skilfully introduced, perhaps accompanied by a deep bow, will express the attitude of penance perfectly.

Besides, what does one do otherwise with certain chants which have been composed recently, like troparies, which are quite big enough to bring the congregation together? Adding a Gloria to them would seem quite superfluous.

Experience also shows that it is interesting when possible to unify all the opening music. Some chants lend themselves to this, those whose verses, strophes or couplets can punctuate each of the minor rituals.

Finally, if you are inclined to take issue with these remarks, it is interesting to note that the Roman *Directory of Masses with Children* (1973) points out: '. . . one should keep in mind that *external activities* will be fruitless and even harmful if they do not serve the *internal participation* of the children' (no. 22). So, 'It is sometimes proper to omit one or other element of the introductory rite or perhaps to enlarge one of the elements' (no. 40).

The document makes things even more precise: 'There should always be at least some introductory element, which is completed by the opening prayer or collect' (no. 40).

This is a valuable indication to all those who have to make pastoral choices, that above all else the Spirit and not the letter of the missal is to be respected.

The whole text of the *Directory* can be found in Appendix 2 of *Celebrating Mass with Children* (see page 107), pp.174–91.

23

Celebrating the Word

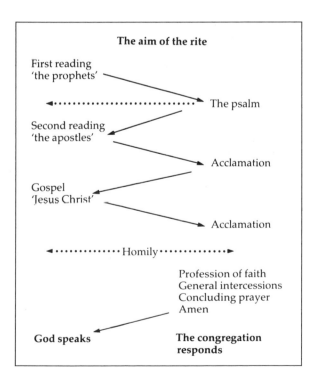

The aim of the rite

First reading
'the prophets'

The psalm

Second reading
'the apostles'

Acclamation

Gospel
'Jesus Christ'

Acclamation

Homily

Profession of faith
General intercessions
Concluding prayer
Amen

God speaks

The congregation responds

This plan, showing how the rite of the word unfolds, is to give us a clearer idea of its aim; the liturgy of the word is a dialogue between God and his people gathered together. An entire liturgy in which one or other of the partners was silent would not be a Christian liturgy.

The plan has deliberately been simplified. For example the psalm is also the word of God, and certain chants which are used as substitutes are as much announcements as responses. As for the homily, it could be placed in both columns: in fact the homilist expands and develops the proclamation and relates it to the present day, at the same time expressing the response of the believer.

There is no certainty that the Bible speaks to us by itself. It was written by and for believers of another age and is often a closed book to us. One does not necessarily read it to find a living word

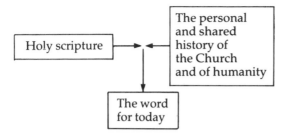

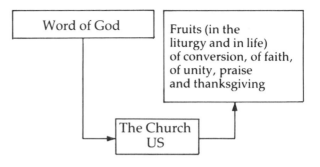

there; that is demonstrated by the number of readers around the world who read it as they would *The Canterbury Tales* or a Shakespeare play!

Besides, we often say that God speaks to us through events. That is true. But how would we be able to hear God in our lives had it not been for the revealed Word, that is to say, Jesus Christ?

It is from the encounter between the Book and life that a word for today springs forth. That is the experience of a Christian who, meditating on the same text at intervals of months or years, finds something new in it: the text has not changed, but he himself, the believer, has gone on living, has grown. The same thing happens in our liturgies: we can hear the same passage from the Bible read every three years or even within the same year, and above all thanks to the homily, the forms of which we shall be looking at later (page 111), for us it is always a word for today, good *news*.

A third diagram will again enable us to see the long-term aim of this rite. It is based on an image from the book of the prophet Isaiah (55.1–11):

For as the rain and the snow come down from heaven,
and return not thither but water the earth,
making it bring forth and sprout,
giving seed to the sower and bread to the eater,
so shall my word be that goes forth from my mouth;
it shall not return to me empty,
but it shall accomplish that which I purpose, and prosper in the thing for which I sent it.

Rooted in the Bible

Our liturgy of the word is rooted in the Bible. In the Old Testament several major texts are a perfect illustration of the purpose of our Church today.

Re-read the passages already mentioned on page 23 which are to do with the assembly, particularly those where the covenant is renewed:
– Joshua 24: Joshua recalls all that YHWH has done for his people and the people again choose YHWH as their God.
– II Kings 23: Josiah reads the book of the Covenant.
– Nehemiah 8: on the return from exile scrolls of the Law are rediscovered. A great liturgy is described in detail. Ezra stands on a wooden platform (our ambo?) where he dominates the people; he 'reads in the book, translating and explaining the meaning: thus people understood the reading' (our homily!).

Our present-day liturgy is also certainly a legacy of the synagogue liturgy. The most significant allusion is one made by the Gospel of Luke (4.16) in which Jesus (a layman) reads from scripture and delivers the homily: 'Today this passage of scripture has been fulfilled.'

In short, in the primitive Christian liturgy one finds these constants:
proclamation, followed by a commentary
the singing of psalms (and hymns)
the prayer by the people
the prayer by the president.

This image of Isaiah has of course been applied throughout the whole Christian tradition to Jesus himself, the Word of God come down from heaven to earth.

And it applies remarkably well to what the liturgy of the word should be in depth. Because just as the Word was made flesh and took on the form of a human body, so too today the word of God takes form in his Church.

But to return to the prophetic image: the word ascends in the fruits of conversion (it is still more obvious in a penitential liturgy), of faith (symbolized by the creed), of unity (one of its manifestations is the general intercessions in which we intercede for all our brothers and sisters), of praise and of thanksgiving (it is still the eucharist, whether or not it is sacramental).

This effectiveness of the word, symbolized through the liturgical rites, is also borne out in the daily life of the believer and of the Church. Thanks to the word, we put our life on God's wavelength; thanks to it, with Christ we carry the burden of our brothers and sisters; thanks to it, we live 'to the praise of God', as the psalms say, or, as St Paul says, we live by 'giving thanks' (Col. 3.15).

God's 'I love you'

Too many liturgies seem to us to be an indigestible string of words threaded together without forethought.

Often, too, those involved do not avoid the pitfall of making their tone either purely catechetical or moralizing or even ideological. Undoubtedly the liturgy of the word does include some elements of catechesis, ethics, doctrine and so on (see page 111), but that is not the essential thing about it.

The liturgy of the word is not even first and foremost sheer information, even if in fact today many of the texts are unfamiliar to the vast majority of worshippers. To take an example: when we hear the gospel of the nativity or the resurrection these are no longer pieces of information for us; we know them almost by heart. As pieces of information, then, they are not up-to-date news. And besides, these texts have been read out every year for twenty centuries.

The 'I love you' of lovers (re-read page 9), constantly repeated, pronounced over and over again, makes their love grow and strengthens their mutual pact; it is not informative but, in specialist jargon, performative, that is to say that it is active, transforming, effective, in a word, creative. And so is God's 'I love you', which is expressed in various scriptural texts. In this way there is a renewal of the covenant, the exchange of a word given and a word received: God and his people do not cease from renewing the mutual consent of their mystical marriage, sealed in the blood of the lamb.

A celebration

The 'I love you' of lovers, particularly on special occasions, is always a festival, and can be accompanied by flowers, presents, even a meal. In the same way the liturgy of the word is a festival, a celebration, and ought to use symbolic actions more than it actually does.

That is why the word of God is proclaimed aloud, why it passes through human lips. Otherwise, with all the means of communication at our disposal we could be content with giving out a piece of paper or a book and saying 'Read this or that'. No, 'I love you' should be spoken aloud.

This declaration of love is the first symbolic step, but we should not forget the other ingredients of the liturgy. Every liturgy of the word is accompanied by gestures: standing for the gospel and kissing the Book as a mark of respect because it represents the pinnacle of revelation; but sometimes also carrying it in solemn procession, acclaiming it (see below), incensing it, raising it up during the creed, and so on. But there is nothing against thinking of other gestures which make the word present, not only to our minds but to our whole being. Those who organize children's worship know this well; but it is often very necessary with adults too.

The visual can find its place, particularly in our picture-conscious civilization. A symbolic picture can support a particular biblical passage, a spotlight can suddenly light up an object, and so on.

But the most usual and most effective ways are undoubtedly music and singing.

The musical environment of the word

The missal provides for singing the psalm and the acclamations, and the possibility of singing for the creed and the general intercessions.

The psalm

Vatican II wanted to give the psalm the important place which the oldest Christian tradition accords it. For a long period that tradition thought of it more as an announcement of the word than as a response of the people (at that time they responded with short phrases or alleluias): 'The responsorial psalm is an integral part of the liturgy of the word' (GIRM 36).

We know the place the psalm holds in the prayer of the Church. Until other forms of celebration are brought back, the Mass is at present the place where worshippers can rediscover its inexpressible richness.

The psalm carries with it the same difficulties as the other biblical texts (pages 104ff.); moreover many people find it difficult to use.

In fact, it would appear that they are ignoring all the flexibility suggested by the missal:

As to content: 'Normally the psalm is taken from the Lectionary, for the texts in it have been chosen so as to have some bearing on it' (GIRM 36). However, in order to make congregational participation easier, one can also use what is called the 'common psalm' for a series of Sun-

days. And it is not against the rules to leave out the more obscure verses or even to replace the psalm with another more suited to the assembly.

One can use a different refrain from that written in the lectionary, provided that it is on the same lines. It can be a refrain or a familiar part of a refrain which holds together musically.

As far as performance goes there are many possibilities. Without going into detail, let me mention just a few. Without requiring the 'psalmist' to have the art of cantillation, the psalm can be spoken rather than read, rather as one recites a poem. A quiet musical background, even if it is only a sustained note or an arpeggiated guitar chord, will help the reader to make it lyrical.

Finally, note that when there is only one reading before the gospel there are three possible schemes: 1. just the psalm; 2. just the acclamation; 3. the psalm and the acclamation (in the last instance be sure to show that there are two quite different approaches, one interiorizing and one externalizing).

The acclamation

To say 'Alleluia, Christ is risen' in the same way as a recorded 'I am sorry that the number that you are dialling does not exist' is not an acclamation but ritualism. The acclamation usually demands to be sung if it is really to be a gesture. During Lent the alleluia is replaced by another acclamation: that gives the Paschal alleluia all the more force. Finally, experience shows that it is interesting to use the same acclamation again at the end of the gospel, which is then enclosed symmetrically within two cries of joy. This is not exactly as laid down, but the spirit is respected even more.

Other possibilities

But there are other possibilities which the missal does not rule out and which experience commends.

First of all the chant.

It is sometimes interesting to open the liturgy of the word with part of a psalm or a refrain; that will often be worth all the 'introductions' that one can do.

From time to time why not begin with a procession of the Bible and an acclamation?

There are certain canticles which can punctuate the whole liturgy of the word.

An interesting line of research is that of the 'chant for the word'. It is very traditional and eminently educative to extend the gospel or finish the homily with a chant. Certain canticles lend themselves to this very well.

Instrumental music is a resource of which full use is not made. Music is able to create space for the word and prayer, for example when in some assemblies it is not possible to have a chant after the reading or at the end of the homily, if, that is, the homily is not 'closed' and is open to internalization. We have seen that an instrument can help the psalm to be more lyrical. It can also sometimes help if a reading is introduced by playing some evocative refrain for all to sing. It is important to use the imagination and utilize the skills of instrumentalists. The use of instruments is too often paralysed, to the great detriment of our congregations and of musicians who are forced to abandon their talents.

Finally, silence. Why rush into the chant at the end of a reading? Is the tempo of the readings the same as the general intercessions? Everything is a matter of rhythm and timing: it is impossible to give firm directions. But the word should be truly broken so that it can mount up again in the profession of faith, in intercession and in praise.

The two tables

It is still very traditional imagery to speak of the liturgy of the word and the eucharistic liturgy as two tables at which the bread of life is shared. This parallel is already suggested by John 6, where the Word introduces himself as food. We are used to the idea of the 'real presence' in the symbols of bread and wine. But are we so keenly aware that 'Christ is present among the faithful through his word' (GIRM 33)?

The comparison between the two tables is a telling one; as the bread and the wine, 'fruits of the earth and the work of human hands', become a sign of the presence of Christ, so do the human words which are the scriptures. And in the same way that the priest has the responsibility of breaking the eucharistic bread among the brethren, so he has to be mindful that the bread of the word is shared (particularly through the homily).

Here are two inseparable tables, to the degree that the first is indispensable to the second. There is no sacrament which is not preceded by a liturgy of the word, even if only in embryo: even when communion is taken to the sick, there is a mini Bible reading. That is to acknowledge the 'close connection between the liturgy of the word and the celebration of the Lord's Supper' (*Eucharisticum Mysterium*, 10).

The psalm

A story: One Sunday I had recited Psalm 141; in the evening, during a meeting of young couples, someone said to me: 'That was a pretty tough text! Who wrote it?'

Now before we give up, let's ask ourselves whether we have given the psalm a fair chance. Isn't it often an extra reading (and badly done) tacked on by the reader to the first reading to the point that one can no longer tell the one from the other? In short, a formality . . .

There's a little trick to give the psalm a fair chance. Often reader A is asked to do the reading and the psalm and reader B to do the second reading: but give the two readings to Mr A and the psalm to Mrs B and see what happens.

Finally, preachers often begin from the Gospel, more rarely from both readings and never from the psalm. However, while being the response of the congregation, the psalm is also the word. And from earliest times it formed an essential element in the liturgy of the word and the expression of the faith.

24

Proclamation

In the readings, the treasures of the Bible are opened to the people; this is the table of God's word (GIRM 34).

When we remember that, for centuries, the Christian people has had to be satisfied with around fifty pericopes (pericope = passage, extract) from the Gospels, and that important texts like the Burning Bush or the Parable of the Prodigal Son were never read on Sundays, we can thank God that Vatican II has opened up the 'treasures of the Bible' to the assemblies again. It is certainly still too early to evaluate the enrichment of faith which the regular reading of these important texts of the Bible brings, and the thirst for better understanding of them to which it has given rise.

The reform has totally reorganized the distribution of the great biblical texts.

On Sundays, the ancient tradition of three readings has been revived: Old Testament ('the prophets'); New Testament ('the apostles') and Gospels, to which must be added the psalm, which is also taken from the Bible. During the week one reading (Old Testament or New Testament) before the Gospel is thought to be enough.

On Sundays, the Synoptic (= parallel) Gospels are distributed over what is called ordinary time following a triennial plan (Year A: Matthew; B: Mark; C: Luke). The Fourth Gospel, that of John, is divided out according to an equally ancient tradition over Lent and Eastertide of the three years. Advent and Lent also use a three-year cycle, but with exceptions dictated by the dynamics particular to these important seasons.

The first reading and the psalm have always been chosen to fit in with the Gospel; for example, each year on the second Sunday in Lent the reading is about the scene of the Transfiguration, where Jesus is claimed to be the well-beloved Son, and the first reading each year recalls a different episode of the covenant which God made with Abraham and his descendants. It also happens that the first reading has been chosen because the Gospel quotes a phrase from it, for example on the second Sunday in Advent B, where Mark quotes Isaiah.

For the second reading there are two kinds of choice:
– for festivals or special occasions it, too, is chosen to fit the Gospel;
– during ordinary time, the option has been made as with the Gospel, for a continuous reading of the epistles (or more precisely a semi-continuous reading, because the books are not in any case read in their entirety). And so in this way we have two continuous readings which inevitably cannot be in harmony except by happy coincidence: that of the Gospel and that of a book of the New Testament.

There are some particularly bad instances: on the fourth ordinary Sunday of Year B, between the announcement of a prophet who will rise up in the midst of the people (Deut. 18.15–20) and the healing of a man possessed (Mark 1.21–18), Paul tells us, with no warning, what he thinks of marriage and celibacy (I Cor. 7.32–35). To put things right it is not enough to say, as did one well-intentioned priest, 'And now for something completely different'!

During the week, save for accidental exceptions, it is important to try to preserve coherence at any price. In practice, on the one hand the three Synoptic Gospels are spread over the year (John is still kept for Eastertide, with Acts) and on the other the rest of the Old and New Testament are spread over a two-year cycle.

But this arrangement is to be treated with considerable pastoral flexibility, as GIRM indicates (319–20):

In the weekday lectionary, readings are provided for each day of the year. Unless a solemnity or feast occurs, these readings are to be used regularly on the days to which they are assigned.

The continuous reading during the week, however, is sometimes interrupted by the occurrence of a feast or particular celebration. In this case the priest should consider in advance the entire week's readings and he may either combine readings so that none will be omitted or decide which readings are to be preferred.

In Masses for special groups, the priest may choose readings suitable for the group, provided they are taken from the texts of an approved lectionary.

The lectionary has a special selection of readings from scripture for Masses in which certain sacraments or sacramentals are celebrated and also for particular circumstances.

These selections provide the people with more suitable readings of God's word and lead them to a fuller understanding of the mystery in which they take part. In this way they are formed in a deeper love of his word.

Pastoral considerations and the permission to choose readings should determine which texts are proclaimed to the assembly.

Experience shows that, for 'God to speak', it is not enough to proclaim all the readings without asking oneself questions. While we have to trust in the rite, this trust cannot be blind to the point of forgetting the congregation to which it is addressed.

It is obvious that the biblical text presents real obstacles to the present-day generation of Christians who have only too recently been put back in contact with the scriptures.

1. Despite the wealth of biblical studies, Catholics as a whole are still largely unfamiliar with the world of the Bible, its language and culture. It will be the role of the homily to reduce that distance. But for the moment certain texts remain closed books, and there is even a risk of their being taken in exactly the opposite sense. Or again it is sometimes the case that the Old Testament text can only be understood after hearing the Gospel.

2. As we have seen, the second reading on ordinary Sundays often breaks the coherence of the liturgy of the word. Note that when I speak of coherence here this coherence is not a matter of Cartesian logic. It is not a matter of reducing the word of God to a theme in the intellectual sense of the term. It is something to be thankful for that the Church asks us to read texts which we would not choose if left to our own devices and by which we should allow ourselves to be provoked.

What pastoral solutions can we find to these problems, while still realizing the ritual plan of the Church?

First of all, we must not forget the flexibility which the missal itself offers us:

> It is strongly recommended that the three readings be used, but for pastoral reasons and by decree of the conference of bishops the use of two readings is allowed in some places. In such a case, the choice between the first two readings should be based on the norms in the lectionary and the desire to lead the people to a deeper knowledge of scripture and never simply because of the brevity or simplicity of the reading (GIRM 318).

Sisters of St Paul of Kinshasa. *Photo E.P.A.*

The effectiveness of the word of God is not a matter of quantity. The *Directory of Children's Masses*, quoted earlier, goes even further (43–45):

If all the readings appointed for a day do not seem suitable for the understanding of children it is permissible to choose readings or a reading either in the lectionary of the missal or directly from the Bible, taking account of the liturgical season. It is, however, suggested that the different Conferences of Bishops should compose lectionaries for children's Masses.

If it seems necessary for the understanding of children to leave out a particular verse in the Bible reading, it should be done carefully and in such a way that one 'does not mutilate the meaning of a text or its spirit or the style of scripture in any way'.

In the choice of readings the criteria must be the quality rather than the brevity of a scriptural text. A short reading is not always intrinsically more suitable for children than a long one. Everything depends on the spiritual use that may be made of the reading.

Since in the biblical text itself 'God addresses his people . . . and Christ himself is there, present by his word, in the midst of the faithful', paraphrases of Holy Scripture are to be avoided. However, the use of existing translations made for the catechesis of children which have been approved by the relevant authority is commended.

Not all our assemblies are capable of digesting three texts. What is the objection to leaving out a small, obscure passage provided that the omission does not upset or distort the general sense? Conversely, some texts from which the lectionary only presents a short reading gain by being read in their entirety. So those who organize the liturgy have to bring to it a pastoral, educational and biblical awareness: neither too much nor too little.

There might be occasions when the same concern for instruction might induce one to rearrange the order of some texts. For example it often happens that a second reading which sits uneasily between the first reading and the gospel can gain in meaning if placed after the homily, which would help the congregation to follow it.

Finally, just because it is felt that some texts should be removed, that does not mean that they should be neglected. Here are some examples: on 1 January, the first reading is a splendid welcome and benediction to open the New Year; the second reading for Palm Sunday (the hymn to the Philippians) makes a marvellous preface when the liturgy of the word needs to be lightened; the first paragraph of the second reading on Good Friday is a perfect introduction

The choice of readers

Some people prefer the readers to be chosen in advance and prepared. Others ask the first to arrive at a given time, with the aim of avoiding any suggestion that one is turning them into functionaries, and of marking the representative character of the person drawn from the congregation.

But which should be the prime consideration, the word or the representative character of the reader? In no way does the congregation benefit when, on the pretext of making sure that it is represented, one runs the risk of readers who are inaudible (which unfortunately happens frequently). The proclamation of the word calls for a technical, spiritual and liturgical competence. That needs to be learned.

It is essential that whatever way of choosing is used, it takes account of the need for an effective proclamation. Otherwise the word is lost.

to the great universal prayers. Finally, where it is practicable, some texts can nourish personal prayer after communion.

Certainly one must guard against disrupting the usual order of the liturgy of the word, because this order has a symbolic meaning (with the Gospel as a climax) and the worshippers need landmarks. But pastoral necessity might occasionally suggest moderate rearrangements which will be welcomed by the congregation provided that one has taken the precaution of explaining to them that it is for a better understanding of God's word.

The reader's task

1. Preparation

Read the text aloud at least once to avoid phonetic traps. Understand the meaning of the text and be familiar with its context in the celebration.

Grasp the overall shape of the text, the linking passage, the climaxes, its point.

2. The reading

Stand comfortably in the appointed place. Look at the congregation while waiting for their attention.

Give the title, e.g., 'A reading from the Second Book of Kings', and function and wait for a moment.

Remember that one always tends to go too quickly. Put yourself in the place of those listeners who are unfamiliar with the passage. Know how to make use of silence. A long silence for the reader is a short one for the listener.

Avoid letting the voice drop at the ends of phrases, or even more at the end of the text: the reading calls for a sequel.

Pronounce final consonants clearly.

Avoid a sing-song tone, which is falsely seductive; a theatrical tone gets in the way of our approach to God.

At the end of the reading do not walk away as if you had just finished a day's forced labour.

3. An art in itself

The reading of liturgical texts differs from normal reading aloud. The reader is not uttering his or her own words but that of God.

Bonhoeffer wrote:

It will soon become apparent that is is not easy to read the Bible aloud for others. The more artless, the more objective, the more humble one's attitude towards the material is, the better will the reading accord with the subject . . . It may be taken as a rule for the right reading of the Scriptures that the reader should never identify himself with the person who is speaking in the Bible. It is not that I am angered, but God; it is not I giving consolation, but God; it is not I admonishing, but God admonishing in the Scriptures. I shall be able, of course, to express the fact that it is God who is angered, who is consoling and admonishing, not by indifferent monotony, but only with inmost concern and rapport, as one who knows that he himself is being addressed. It will make all the difference between right and wrong reading of Scriptures if I do not identify myself with God but quite simply serve him. Otherwise I risk . . . directing attention to myself instead of to the Word. But this is to commit the worst of sins in presenting the Scriptures . . . (Life Together, SCM Press and Harper 1954, ch. 2).

That is why the Eastern Churches have always had the readings sung.

The readings

It is best to keep to the passages laid down by the lectionary in order to maintain the link with the universal Church. On the other hand they can be used with more flexibility. For example, do not hesitate to read the same passage twice (this is a worthwhile exercise, too, with children):

1. An 'ordinary' reading of the passage
2. Homiletic reflection.
3. Solemn proclamation.

Or begin with 3 and end with a meditative reading of all or part of it.

The place of the word

Just as the eucharistic table occupies a privileged place, so too does the table of the word. GIRM emphasizes that 'the lectern or ambo should be a fixed pulpit and not a simple movable stand' (272). In antiquity the ambo was a kind of small platform surrounded by a rail, usually built at the junction of the choir and the nave.

This architectural symbol cannot always be put into practice, but the idea of a fixed and solid place is an important one. It goes with the sense of symbolism in space: a place for each action. And just as in a church you do not put the altar in a corner after the Mass, so too the place from which the reading is given remains as a witness to what has been proclaimed there and will be proclaimed again.

Besides, GIRM lays down that 'the readings, responsorial psalm, and *Exsultet* are proclaimed from the lectern' and that 'it may be used also for the homily and general intercessions (prayer of the faithful)'. And it goes on to add, 'It is less suitable for the commentator, cantor or choirmaster to use the lectern.'

25

The Homily

In curious contrast to the usual liturgical jargon, this word really has become popular. It is true that the old terms have regrettable connotations which tell us a good deal about a certain kind of preaching: 'preach' has given us 'preachy' and 'sermon' has given us 'sermonize'. Does the success of the word 'homily' perhaps indicate a desire for change? But too often, people are unaware of the ideal represented by this word.

It comes from a Greek word, *homilein*, meaning 'to converse familiarly with'. The size of our congregations means that the listeners can no longer ask questions very often, and that is a pity. This was the custom at Corinth, for example (read I Cor. 14.34f., where Paul quite rightly forbids women to interrupt and tells them to wait until they get home to ask questions of their husbands. Different customs in different ages!). One does not come across it today except among small congregations or with children. A shared homily or a sharing of the gospel also comes very close to this idea. Thank God – and perhaps also thanks to modern means of amplification – many homilies are at least able to rediscover this style of familiar conversation.

A still more important consideration is that the word homily indicates a content: 'it should develop some point of the readings or of another text from the Ordinary or the Mass of the day. The homilist should keep in mind the mystery that is being celebrated and the needs of the particular community' (GIRM 41). The affirmation is clear: the homily is closely tied to scripture and in a broader sense to the mystery of the day. If it is not, let us call a spade a spade and not dignify with the name of homily a sermon on abortion or on the missions to Patagonia, even if the preacher goes into contortions to pin what he is saying artificially on to snatches of scripture.

As a commentary on scripture the homily can and should cover several aspects which can be briefly summarized here:

– to explain scripture (exegesis) by clarifying a particular term, a particular historical situation, a particular obscure passage;

– to make them topical ('today this word is fulfilled') for the particular congregation, whatever it is and whatever its life-style; that is to say, to exercise one's pastoral sense;

– to proclaim the paschal mystery of which every word is an integral part (kerygma);

– to teach (catechesis) every aspect of the history of salvation;

– to explain the meaning of sacramental signs (mystagogy);

– to help in deciphering God's plan for us here and now, to look for the signs of the kingdom, to welcome the future which God is preparing for us and which he calls on us to prepare with him (prophecy);

– to bear witness, whether it be by personal involvement ('you and me') or by showing an example of the way in which the faith is lived out (what happens in life) or by occasionally using individual Christians or groups of Christians as an example:

– then the final duty of a homilist, often commended by St Paul, is to exhort and encourage.

Obviously, not all these dimensions can be present and explicit in each homily. But it is the responsibility of the priest or the pastoral team to make sure that, over a period, for example during the course of a year, all these functions of a homily are covered. It is up to them, too, to see that homilies do not become moralistic, or authoritarian, or drily doctrinal and divorced from life, or paternalistic. It is up to them to see that individuals do not constantly ride their favourite hobby horses. It will not be difficult to ensure this if one listens to members of the congregation and encourages them to react or, even better, if one gets the liturgical team to comment on one another.

The position of the homily

The homily traditionally comes after the gospel. But two things are worth noting:

1. It is sometimes useful from a teaching point of view to bring it forward if one of the two readings has provided its starting point or been an essential reference point. The homily could also be profitably split up into several interruptions during the liturgy of the word, so long as care is taken not to give the impression that one is preaching several times.

2. The introductions to the readings – the famous 'headings' drawn up by the liturgical

Photo Rémy Tournus

team (and even certain interpolations during the rest of the liturgy) are also a kind of homily. The important thing is that they should not be a précis of what is about to be read. (One is constantly being told 'As St Paul will tell us . . .' Let him speak for himself!) And like the homily, these interpolations should contain the biblical facts necessary for a proper understanding or, by a question-and-answer method, they should stimulate the attention by suggesting a link between the word and daily living. In short, our words should not do a disservice to the word, but serve it.

What is the purpose of the homily?

In accord with ancient tradition the homily is entrusted to an ordained minister. Vatican II still prescribes: 'The homily should ordinarily be given by the celebrant' (GIRM 60). The same person breaks the bread of the word and the eucharistic bread.

There are of course obvious reasons which often prevent us from observing this recommendation. At the very least the organization should avoid what I call the 'clock-tower marathon', where the preacher only appears for the homily, to disappear again immediately afterwards.

There are even exceptional cases where the homily ought to be entrusted to a lay man or woman, not only in house groups where no priest can be present, but also for several subjects which need to be preached about where a lay person would be more competent than the priest himself.

But in all circumstances, in the spirit of the Church, the homily will always be given under the auspices of the pastoral ministry.

In certain small or very homogeneous congregations a sharing of the word would be ideal. That could range from the simple quotation of a phrase which has struck each of the participants to a more detailed exchange. However, the president's role is not just to leave people to it: first of all he offers any necessary explanations in order to prevent the faithful from straying into false interpretations; then he keeps a watching brief while everyone makes his or her own contribution, intervening to shed light where necessary, and so on. Certainly, too, at the end of the time of sharing he should gather together in a united prayer all the riches to which the Spirit has given birth.

From where should the homily be given?

'The homily is given at the chair or from the lectern' (GIRM 97). The lectern or the place of the word is certainly the most usual place. A homily given from a chair may surprise a modern reader. However, in ancient times the bishop addressed the faithful from a sitting position, while they usually remained standing (!). One can imagine this still happening today in the case of the bishop, but a priest! However, it could happily occur in small groups.

In this it is necessary to take note of two things which are not necessarily contradictory: 1. a place which is in some way stable and customary, and 2. a place which facilitates communication.

In conclusion, most Christians listen attentively to the homily, thank God. It is up to those responsible to see that it is in harmony with the rest of the liturgy, and that calls for close collaboration between the person giving the homily and those responsible for the worship. Let the bread of the word be truly shared as 'nourishment of the Christian life' (GIRM 41).

26

Response to the Word

The profession of faith

In the profession of faith or creed the people have the opportunity to respond and give assent to the word of God which they have heard in the readings and the homily. It is also a time for the people to recall the teachings of the faith before they begin to celebrate the eucharist (GIRM 43).

Situated as it is after the homily and before the general intercessions, the creed is *de facto* a good response to the first of these two aims; the second, which is also traditional (see the box) runs a great risk of being only a pious intention, unless one allows oneself an occasional reversal of the order.

This profession of faith is something in which all the people join, as well as the priest.

It seems that singing such a doctrinal text goes against modern susceptibilities. That is why here and there attempts have been made to punctuate the saying of it with refrains, thereby going back to a very old tradition without realizing it. It is no longer forbidden to use the question and answer form provided for baptism or the Easter vigil.

Let us also recognize that the Nicene Creed often seems rather overloaded. Hence some things would seem desirable:

More general use of the Apostles' Creed, which is shorter and above all more biblical, and closer to the original kerygma than one finds in a number of passages in the New Testament (kerygma = paschal proclamation; read for example Acts 2.22–23; 3.13–17; 10.39–40);

Occasionally the recitation of the creed might be replaced with a more detailed profession of faith, more in keeping with the mystery of the day.

It might even be omitted, if the response to the word is expressed in another equally significant way (for example 'the chant for the word', page 103).

Besides, the great profession, the rule of faith, is not only expressed but put into action in the eucharistic prayer itself.

Furthermore, there is often a risk that the creed will interrupt the flow of the liturgy of the word. Over the centuries its place has varied; in many liturgies it came at the beginning of the eucharist. Vatican II did not want to upset our usual routine.

To sum up, it is good and significant if we regularly recite the rule of faith with our fellow Christians everywhere and always and in this way identify ourselves with the faith of the Church, with and in spite of our difficulties in believing, not to mention our doubts. But it is necessary to remind ourselves frequently of the significance of the rite, so that the creed does not become a routine gesture, sometimes just a signal . . . for the collection to be taken.

God says to his people, 'I love you', and they give him their loyalty: 'I believe in you because you love us.' That is the ultimate aim of this rite and that is what it means.

The general intercessions

The general intercessions are one of the most obvious results of Vatican II reform. The Church has been without this rite since at least the sixth century, except on Good Friday. Some of the intercessions are still reminiscent of the prayers of the prone (where prayers were said, among others, 'for our sons under the colours', i.e. serving in the army): that was a relic of the old general intercessions.

The general intercessions are also called the 'prayer of the faithful'. This is a fitting title because 'In the general intercessions . . . the people exercise their priestly function by interceding for all mankind' (GIRM 45).

Therefore it is quite legitimate that in some places the shaping of this prayer is left to lay people (but it should not be supposed that they have 'prepared' the liturgy by limiting themselves to this task!).

The missal lays down the content as follows: 'Intercession for the Church, for civil authorities, for those oppressed by various needs, for all mankind, and for the salvation of the world.'

Vast horizons, commensurate with the size of God's heart. A framework into which all categories of human beings, all human situations and all the happenings of our present-day world can be put, the general intercessions are an opportunity for our congregations. So that the best possible use can be made of them, attention needs to be given to their form and content.

The missal suggests four main areas: 'the needs of the Church, public authorities and the salvation of the world, those oppressed by any need, the local community.'

Some people stick so doggedly to this plan that it becomes artificial. Others have quite rightly grasped that this prayer introduces all the tumult of the world into our Church, in which case the general intercessions run the risk of becoming a spoken newspaper which keeps us abreast of events. The rite is threatened with yet other digressions: that of moralism ('Let us pray, brothers and sisters, that we may be more loving towards one another', the implication being that *you* (the people) are not sufficiently so); or the temptation for the preacher to use it to summarize the points of his homily!

In connection with the first group, it is worth

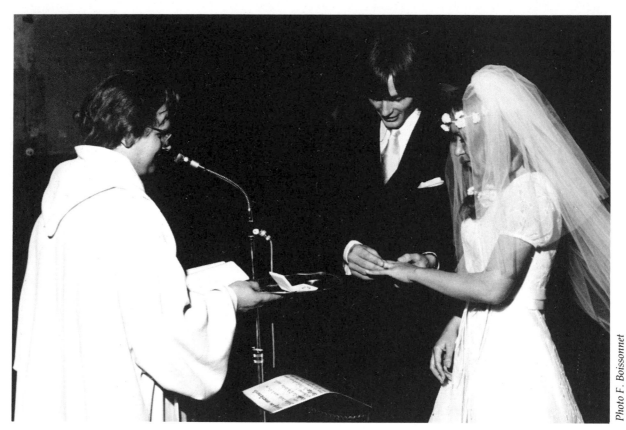

God says to his people, 'I love you', and that is what binds them together: 'I believe in you because you love us.'

remembering that the Church has provided us with a plan. It is not obligatory that each main intention should be formulated on every Sunday, but if one normally prays in these four areas the value of the prayer as a whole will be felt over a succession of Sundays.

Those who fall into the trap of giving a newspaper report, or into that of moralism, should remember that in prayer one is speaking primarily to God. Think back to the great solemnity of the old litanies: 'Deliver us from all evil . . . That it may please thee to bring among the peoples sincere understanding and peace, grace, Hear us, good Lord . . .' It is probable that the structure of the 'For . . . that . . .' in the first formulas suggested by the Council have tended to make us tell God how he must act: he is too great for that. And that brings us to the form . . .

116

The creed: a complicated history

Originally the creed was a profession of faith drawn up for the liturgy of baptism, as the Apostles' Creed still is today.

The creed known as the Niceno-Constantinopolitan Creed, which has a less biblical structure and contains more abstract theological expressions, made its appearance early on in the evolution of the Mass, where it seems to have been introduced mainly through a zeal for orthodoxy in the face of the heresies that shook the Eastern Churches. But at the time it was placed after the prayer of the faithful (our general intercessions) as a starting point for the eucharistic liturgy.

Popularized during the eleventh century in the West through the pressure from the Emperor Hernry II, it was increasingly thought of as a solemn element and for this reason was used on Sundays and festivals. It is interesting to note that in the East the creed is normally recited either by everyone or by a representative of the congregation (not a priest) and that it is never sung. By contrast, in the West it has always been thought of as a hymn of the people, a principle forgotten during the time of polyphonic, and later symphonic, Masses, of which it was often the *pièce de résistance*.

Assemblies without a priest

The general intercessions – the profession of faith
It is interesting to reverse the usual order: in this way the general intercessions form a happy link with the gospel that has been read and the creed again takes the place which it had in ancient times, as the hinge between the rite of the word and the eucharist.

Nevertheless, if you keep to the order of the missal, you can mix praise with supplication in the great Judaeo-Christian tradition, following this pattern for each section of praise:
We bless you, Lord, for . . .
Remember . . . or, We pray for . . .

Spontaneous interventions

Since the general intercessions are the prayer of the faithful, it is logical to go all the way and allow them to intervene freely. But this practice does have its problems, especially in large congregations where relations between people are less well defined. So some precautions must be taken:

First of all, pin up written intentions where everyone can see them:

Then – and this is the role of the priest, the representative man – try to broaden the individual intentions that are offered. For example, if someone asks for a prayer on behalf of a family which is financially deprived, the priest can then enlarge on this, perhaps by including all those in the world who do not have the necessities of life, and also for those who are struggling for justice and dignity for humankind ('The priest presides over the prayer',

GIRM 47).

In some places the difficulty of particularity in prayers has been overcome by having a book in which each person can write his or her intentions. This is placed at the back of the church, and brought up at the time of the general intercessions: or perhaps the priest can sum up the intentions in the spirit of what is said in the book, or perhaps the symbolic gesture of carrying up the book would be sufficient.

NB If the list is not too long, the names of those who have been baptized or married, or who have died, during the week are better mentioned during the intercessions of the eucharistic prayer. But if they are mentioned here, care must be taken to put them in a wider context.

How should the general intercessions be put into words?

This rite has very quickly become fossilized. Inevitably we have 'Let us pray to God' and the clumsiness of 'for . . . that he may', which is not English, but a translation of the Latin. It is vital for this mechanism to be broken at least from time to time for the meaning to be revived. Is it always necessary to say 'Let us pray to God' if the commentator and the organist or musicians have the text in front of them? And then one should speak in English. Our language favours short phrases and does not go in for subordinate clauses. Instead of saying, 'We pray for our Church, beset by the problems of the times, that God may give it his strength', say, 'Lord, you see our Church. It is faced with so many problems. Help it.'

And why not begin each intention with a benediction to echo what the Gospel has said? For example, 'You are blessed, Lord, who cured the man born blind. Open our eyes.' The basic progression of biblical and Christian prayer is that of the Psalms, the Our Father and the eucharistic prayer.

Try also to find a universal language. The way things are put, especially where political divisions or local conflicts are involved, can divide people instead of drawing them together. Remember that symbolic language has a better chance of unifying people over a disagreement: if a local firm is in difficulties pray 'for all those who suffer anxiety over the future', and that will be to pray for the boss trying to save the firm as much as for those whose salaries are threatened by unemployment.

It is normal for a refrain to be inserted after each intention. This has the advantage that it can fit in with the mystery of the day; if the liturgy is reminding us of God's faithfulness, a refrain of 'You are the eternally faithful God' or 'Lord, we trust in your love' will be of more value than all the hackneyed repetitions which tend to appear. But the missal also suggests that supplication can be conveyed 'by silent prayer' (GIRM 47). This assumes that the intercessor will give his or her fellow-worshippers time to add their own particular concerns; and that he or she will pray sincerely, will find an agreeable tone of voice and pace, and in addition will avoid the hectoring tone too often found in this rite.

The general intercessions as a profession of faith!

Prayer is also an act of faith: 'You have told us that you save us and we believe this. Now, Lord, save us today from this and that.'

The general intercessions open our hearts to the wideness of the heart of Christ who dies 'for the people'. It is the congregation's answer to the word which they have heard on that particular Sunday. Someone has said: 'To prepare the general intercessions you need to have open on the table a Bible on one side and a newspaper on the other.' An imaginative way of indicating from where prayer should draw its inspiration.

27

'Do This in Remembrance of Me'

'And as they were eating, he took bread, and blessed, and broke it, and gave it to them, and said, "Take, this is my body." And he took a cup, and when he had given thanks he gave it to them, and they all drank of it. And he said to them, "This is my blood of the covenant, which is poured out for many."'

This narrative of the institution of the eucharist is taken from the Gospel of Mark (ch. 14). All the particulars can be found in the other versions (Matt. 26; Luke 22; I Cor. 11). They can also be found, with variations in detail, in all our eucharists.

What do we know about the circumstances of the event? In essence, that Jesus instituted the eucharist during a paschal meal, thus bringing about the new covenant which he celebrated before living it out (cf. the paschal liturgy).

Now we know that a Jewish meal, and particularly a paschal meal, was always preceded by an act of thanksgiving, a blessing over the bread and wine. As one of our eucharistic prayers runs, 'Giving thanks, he blessed God.' The two verbs are synonymous, and denote what the Jews called *berakah* and what the New Testament calls *eucharistia*. It is more than a simple thank-you. It is an exchange between God and his people: God is meditated upon and praised; the wondrous things he has done are remembered (see below for *anamnesis*, and he is marvelled at. In Greek, *eucharistein* (*eu* = good; *charis* = grace, favour) means something like 'how beautiful, how good is the gift that you give us!').

And to be sure, after this praise the requests of the day come naturally: there is always the same progression in Judaeo-Christian prayer.

Thus just as the liturgy of the word is rooted in the liturgy of the synagogues (see page 100), so the 'Lord's Supper' is rooted in the paschal meal. The eucharist did not drop from heaven, but is the work of a God who is so fully human that he uses the religious and ritual realities of the people among whom he is incarnate.

The narratives of the institution present a series of distinct actions with a schematic dryness. But the liturgy is never just a copy (except perhaps for the foot-washing?) and over the centuries the Churches have taken up the actions of Christ by using them in the time and form appropriate to their cultural and spiritual age.

So we can translate all Christ's actions into the actions of the liturgy which we have today:

he took the bread . . . the cup	the preparation of the gifts
he gave thanks, he blessed it	eucharistic prayer
he broke it	fraction
and gave it to them	communion

Let us look at each of these rites.

28

He Took Bread and Wine

At the beginning of the liturgy of the eucharist, the gifts which will become the Lord's body and blood are brought to the altar.

First the altar, the Lord's table, is prepared as the centre of the eucharistic liturgy. The corporal, purificator, chalice and missal are placed on it.

The offerings are then brought forward: it is desirable for the faithful to present the bread and wine which are accepted by the priest or deacon at a suitable place. These are placed on the altar with the accompanying prayers. The rite of carrying up the gifts continues the spiritual value and meaning of the ancient custom when the people brought bread and wine for the liturgy from their homes.

This is also the time to bring forward or to collect money or gifts for the poor and the Church. These are to be laid in a suitable place but not on the altar (GIRM 49).

The offertory is an important moment in eucharistic devotion: we are being invited to offer God our 'sacrifices', with the emphasis very much on the personal contributions of our lives and work. In France on May Day workmen's tools used to be brought to the altar.

What is its true value?

Some historical facts

A few historical facts about its origin may

enlighten us. In the first two centuries, at least, this rite was extremely sober, perhaps to dissociate it from pagan sacrifices and to emphasize that there is only one offering, the spiritual offering of Christ to the Father. 'Then bread and . . . wine are brought to the president and taking them he sends up praise and eucharists' (= 'thanksgivings to the Father') writes Justin in his First Apology (65). But gradually the idea of the offering in the sense that we understand it today came to the fore: that of making a gift to God of part of our possessions and therefore of ourselves, of separating ourselves from them, dispossessing ourselves of them, and thus recognizing that all gifts come from God and above all experiencing the joy of bringing to the altar what is to become the sacrifice of Christ. In fact the bread which was brought then was household bread . . . It is clear that this oblation was a duty of all baptized people, linked to their priestly calling. It is the priest who consecrates, but all the people of God who offer the sacrifice with him. Anything left over from the offering was distributed either to the priests or to the poor, under the supervision of the deacons, whose essential function this was.

An offertory procession came into being which, in the East, developed in scale and became known as the 'great entrance' (the little entrance takes place at the beginning of the Mass). It is significant that the chants and prayers of this rite already acclaim the king of glory. To our Cartesian minds this seems illogical, because the bread and wine are not yet consecrated, but it shows how closely the preparation of gifts is bound up with the eucharist proper. An example of liturgical text can be found in the chant 'You only are holy, you only are the Lord', adapted from a chant in the Liturgy of John Chrysostom.

It is unfortunate that subsequently the offertory procession ended up by becoming detached from the sequence of offertory, eucharist and communion. This was above all true in the West towards the tenth century when, under the influence of various theological currents, the use of unleavened bread (as in the Jewish passover) became common. This, of course, could no longer be made at home. At the same time the reception of communion became rarer. The one doubtless explains the other and vice versa.

The survival of the offerings of the faithful is to be found in the collection or in the blessing of the bread. An 'offering' made so to speak as payment for a Mass is another relic of this rite.

As for the spiritual significance of the offertory, it became a kind of parallel to the eucharistic offering (the term host, which in Latin (*hostia*) means victim, is a sign of this trend) and in a laudable but misguided effort it underwent the growth and shift in meaning that we noticed at the beginning.

It is undoubtedly in an effort to re-establish the true aim of this rite that the missal of Paul VI now calls it 'the preparation of the gifts', a more neutral and pragmatic term. The word 'offertory' now appears only in expressions like 'offertory hymn' and 'offertory antiphon'. Let's take the General Instruction of the Missal step by step.

'First the altar, the Lord's table, is prepared as the centre of the eucharistic liturgy.'

The suggestion here is of a profoundly symbolic gesture which relates to our everyday rituals. 'Would you like to come to the table,' says the hostess. And what is more representative and meaningful when one has worked together than laying the table? Why should it not be the same for the eucharistic meal? To do this it is not enough to put down the corporal, that piece of linen reduced to a 40cm square. At least on some special occasions (Christmas, Holy Saturday – Good Friday is already provided for), why not spread out the linen straight away and later put flowers and candles on it, the altar having been

The Last Supper. Hans Holbein the Younger. Basle. *Photo Giraudon*

left bare until then?

This gesture is an apt indication of the symbolism of the 'two tables' (page 103). It makes clear that a second event is taking place, and the gesture of laying the table says a good deal.

Finally, the missal's suggestion shows that this point is also a kind of overture to the eucharistic action, as is the great entrance in the Byzantine rite. We shall come back to this when we consider the hymn.

It is important to give meaning and life to the offertory procession. Here are a few suggestions: all the altar breads that will be needed should be brought up (not taking account of the Reserved Sacrament), and if not the cloth, at least the flowers and the candles. If time has been found to take the collection (see page 127), that can be brought up, too, but not put on the altar (this is a good thing, because in some areas of Africa people bring up goats and chickens!). In some cases, for instance when the collection consists of clothing or provisions, something representative could be taken up. In this way the procession takes on dignity, especially if the faithful, laden with gifts, walk slowly and hold them out in a graceful gesture of offering and do not hurry over it. For the significance of the gesture re-read pages 61ff.

Assemblies without a priest

When possible, and it often is in our huge churches – the congregation ought to face in another direction. To go back to our comparison, after the aperitif or the seminar, by moving to the table the company takes up a new position. One can therefore celebrate the word in one place and then, carrying the bread and wine in procession, move towards the altar.

The journey of the bread

The rite of carrying up the gifts continues the spiritual value and meaning of the ancient custom when the people brought bread and wine for the liturgy from their homes.

Why this insistence on ritual? Because the procession – this movement from below upwards – is an essential part of the symbolism of the eucharist. The eucharist is an exchange between God and humankind in Jesus Christ, as this offertory prayer bears witness:

Blessed are you, Lord, God of all creation. Through your goodness we have this bread to offer

GOD ——————————————→ HUMANKIND

which earth has given
and human hands have made.

←——————————————————

It will become for us the bread of life.

——————————————————————————→

This procession is the first stage of what might be called 'the journey of the bread'.

And it is symmetrical with the communion procession in which those who are to distribute it come to the altar. The symmetry will be all the more obvious if the members of the congregation who bring up the gifts are the same people who help the priest in the distribution of the bread.

There are three main spiritual axes during the time of the offertory.

'Blessed are you, Lord, God of all creation. Through your goodness we have this bread to offer . . . and this wine.'

Like the traditional Jewish meal, our meal begins with a blessing. We remember that everything we have and everything that we do comes from God, the Father Creator of heaven and earth. The first aspect of the offertory is to recognize God as the source of all things.

'Which earth has given and human hands have made.'

It is the mission of the priestly people as a whole to offer to God all creation and all humankind. It still has to be saved: it is Christ who by the gift of himself reconciles the universe.

124

'*This* bread and *this* wine', not just bread and wine. That is to say, it is something of ours, something which comes from ourselves, which we sacrifice, not in the pagan sense of the word, to obtain favours as a *quid pro quo*, but in the sense of something we give up. Because we run the risk of letting things possess us, if we do not rid ourselves of them. Because above all, once more, they come from God and we only have the management of them.

The offering of self is a matter of offering oneself in an even deeper way. Through the gifts that we give it is the Church which offers herself so that God will encompass her in her eagerness to offer and so that she may thus be transfigured into his body.

Finally, although this dimension may not be clearly apparent in the prayers, there is traditionally an idea of sharing in the rite. The bread and the wine are offered so that they can be shared out in the communion. In the same way the various collections are distributed for the needs of the Church (local, diocesan or universal) or for the poor. It is the same again in our lives.

Obviously all these dimensions cannot be brought out in each eucharist, but one or other will be highlighted, depending on the overall context of the Mass.

Great flexibility is allowed to those responsible for the preparation of gifts over what is said or sung in connection with it. If there is neither chant nor music, it follows that the priest will use the verbal formulas laid down (but he does not have to say aloud the private prayers which accompany the pouring of the drop of water, the hand-washing and the bowing).

But it is all to the good if a chant or musical instruments are possible. In fact, after the solemnity of the liturgy of the word, the rite of the preparation of the gifts can be made a more relaxed time which can usefully be filled by a piece of organ music, an anthem sung by the choir or even a congregational hymn. In this case the priest must not compete with the musicians since, according to the missal, he may, but does not need to, say the prayers of presentation aloud.

In the sung repertoire, hymns of an earlier generation, still stamped by the piety of the ancient offertory, must be abandoned. In contrast, many of the hymns of thanksgiving and the psalms of praise well express the recognition that 'everything comes from him and everything is through him', and above all they have the advantage of offering up the praise contained in the opening of the eucharist. For example, the Magnificat can be used here at a Marian feast, the

---

Bread and wine, symbols of great riches

We saw on page 3 the importance of bread in symbolism. In the same way, wine also suggests sharing. Moreover it conjures up joy, festivity, plenty, though also orgies, excess, evil.

For the people of the Bible the meaning was even richer. The Old Testament speaks of the bread of Wisdom, the figure who carries out the plan of God, who spreads the table for those who wish to feed on the divine intelligence. It speaks also of manna, the bread which came down from heaven.

This is the background to John 6, where Jesus presents himself as 'the bread which came down from heaven': he gave his word and flesh as eternal food.

Wine, in the Old Testament, symbolizes plenty and fertility. The cup to be drunk is sometimes bitter, the plan of God whose commands have to be carried out, but it is also the cup of blessing. It is the new wine, the messianic joy and the radical newness of the kingdom which will burst the old wineskins. All the symbolism of the vineyard should also be recalled. So it was not by chance that Jesus took wine to celebrate the new covenant.

Greal Hallel for an Easter eucharist. This line of research ties up with the aspect of the beginning of the eucharist which we can see in these rites.

Perhaps to a greater extent than any other, this moment in our eucharists depends more on the quality of the actions than on the number of words. A simple act to perform, it can be rich in meaning. A less important rite, and the weakest

moment in our worship, it is nonetheless indispensable to the balance and therefore to the wider meaning of our eucharist. The preparation of the gifts is also the preparation of our hearts to join themselves to the unique offering, that of our Lord.

Unleavened or leavened bread? Red or white wine?

Although it is certain that Jesus used unleavened bread, in the early Church leavened bread was brought from home. People simply chose bread which had a good shape and appearance.

Towards the tenth century the return of unleavened bread (not leavened means that it was the bread of travellers, the bread of the exodus) did a great deal of damage to the meaning of the offertory. At the same time, when theologians were getting worked up over the real presence, this bread became more a bread to contemplate, a host to adore, than a bread to share out and eat. It then assumed a round shape (full but flat) and its white form (whiteness, an ambivalent sign of purity) in which we know it, a form which has nourished a complete and sometimes suspect devotional literature.

We shall see in due course the Church's directions for the breaking of bread (page 136).

As for wine, it is for purely practical reasons that some prefer white (it does not stain the linen so much), but the choice is there. The only requirement is that it should be 'the fruit of the vine, natural and pure, having no foreign substances mixed in with it'.

Incense

Having offered up the gifts, the priest may incense them as well as the altar and the people. In this way the Church's offering and its prayer goes up as incense to the presence of God.

'Asking for Masses'

The practice of making an offering of money for a personal intention is a very old one and is justifiable in as much as one does not claim to capitalize on the fruits of the eucharistic sacrifice for oneself – how could one do that?

But it is painful to hear of fees being talked of, as if one were at a solicitor's or doctor's, to read the tariffs of Masses posted up in the sacristy and to have good Christians ask you, 'How much is that?' 'How much do I owe you?' And does the act of asking for Masses without ever being present at them have anything to do with the real Christian meaning of the offertory? I do not want to judge people's faith, but such a practice smacks of paganism.

This whole vocabulary, this whole way of doing things, has very deep roots. Nor is it any secret that dioceses cannot afford to give up this source of income.

Be this as it may, everything should be done in respect of both language and practice to encourage the offerings of the faithful, thereby giving them a better sense of the eucharist.

Sisters of St Paul of Kinshasa. *Photo E.P.A.*

The collection

Is it a sacrament since, as the priest said humourously, it is a tangible and effective sign? No. A liturgical action? Yes, unless for valid reasons it is only taken at the end of the service.

But everything depends on how it is done. In too many churches, even now, the collection goes on long after the offertory and God knows that many Christians are disgusted at the clink of coins around the altar. This is not because they question the meaning and necessity of the gesture – they are often the most generous – but because they are worried on the one hand about the quality of the prayer and on the other about the kind of image this sort of thing gives the Church.

Is it important to have a collection? If it is, then care should be taken to see that it is done well. It is not difficult to arrange it so that it takes as little time as possible: enough baskets should be ready and a sufficient number of collectors. If the bread and wine are brought up in procession, it is even better for the procession to be held back until the collection is finished so that the collectors can join up with this procession. The priest must be ready and waiting. Is everyone convinced of the absolute necessity for a collection? Then is it too much to ask for a few minutes be set aside for it while the organ plays – or perhaps the notices could be given out?

Sisters of St Paul of Kinshasa. *Photo E.P.A.*

Associated rites

The lavabo

After he has offered the bread and wine to God and incensed, if that is required, the priest washes his hands while reciting in a low voice a verse from Ps. 50: 'Wash me throughly from my iniquity, and cleanse me from my sin.' Before Vatican II he recited from Ps. 25 'I will wash my hands in innocence', in Latin *Lavabo manus meas*, which has given its name to this small rite.

There seems to be a double origin for it: the first is practical, since the priest's hands are soiled after receiving the gifts in kind; the second is spiritual, because in some old traditions hands were washed as a sign of inner purification, even before private prayer.

Only this second dimension remains today. But we can well wonder at the expressive value of a gesture which consists of moistening the finger tips with three drops of water!

The drop of water mixed with the wine

There are possibly also two origins of this: some people think that the wines of ancient times were too rich to be drunk without the addition of water. But it cannot be denied that this gesture very quickly took on a spiritual significance: the union of Christ with his people, or, in the context of the controversy surrounding the dogma of the two natures of Christ, the union of humanity and divinity. The private prayer which today accompanies this ritual holds the two meanings together. As with the lavabo it remains to be seen whether this symbolism has anything to say to a Christian of the twentieth century!

The prayer over the gifts

A presidential prayer which concluded the preparation of the gifts, it very quickly came to be said in private (hence the old name 'secret'). Vatican II made it a public prayer, but it often seems superfluous. It is a small administrative problem which has not been sorted out.

29

He Gave Thanks

Leaving aside the old Roman canon, the nine eucharistic prayers instituted by Vatican II are all designed more or less according to the same plan. Here are the various elements, which we shall be looking at in detail:

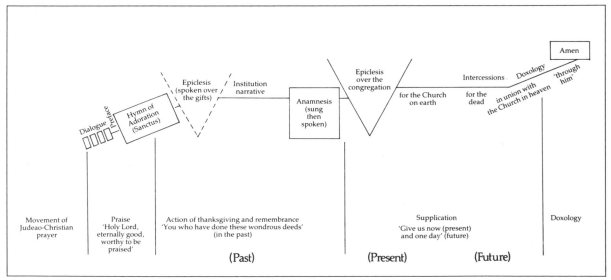

To bless, praise, give thanks, make eucharist: all these terms are more or less synonymous, including the word 'bless', which must be taken in its original sense of 'speak well' of someone (Latin *benedicere*) and not in today's sense of asking for grace to be given.

We saw in the introductory pages on the eucharist that the desire to praise is rooted in biblical prayer. Praising, blessing, giving thanks, making eucharist are all quite different from saying thank you. To say thank you is to convey gratitude, but in the hope of receiving other favours. This is how it is in pagan religions and often in our social relationships. Here, in the eucharist, it is a matter of looking upon Another without ulterior motives, with admiration for the wonders that he has done.

Unless this subtle but essential distinction is understood, you will never be able to get to the heart of the eucharist (not that one can ever fully comprehend it, because 'great is the mystery of faith').

Praise is the starting point for the eucharistic prayer called the 'preface' (a word which here has the meaning of public proclamation). In Eucharistic Prayer IV this praise extends far beyond the preface and encompasses the whole story of the wonders of salvation.

The culmination of God's wondrous works, the wonder of wonders, is certainly Jesus, the Son of God, the Lord and the gift which he made of himself for the salvation of humankind. And (after a detour in the shape of the epiclesis on the gifts) this praise ends in the institution narrative, where this sacrifice of Christ is spoken of in detail.

The sacrifice of praise

Giving thanks, praise, making eucharist, is always recognizing that everything comes from God, that it is he who is active 'at all times and in all places'. It is therefore to give up for oneself

any control of the world, to give up one's own self, to take the spotlight off oneself. That is why, in the context of the eucharist, praising is synonymous with offering and consecrating. It is what the Old Testament calls the sacrifice of praise. Jesus was a living and complete eucharist, having no other purpose than that of doing the will of the Father. This giving up of himself in an outpouring of himself which brought him to the Father (and to us) constitutes his sacrifice. Jesus did not offer words, did not pray half-heartedly, but consecrated himself to his mission and his praise, his eucharist, and that led him to the fate we know. The Mass is not a sacrifice in the pagan sense of the word, a sacrifice when a victim is slain to placate the gods, but a spiritual (and therefore total) offering of love.

Do this in remembrance of me

The eucharist is also a memorial, if we take this in the best sense of the word (and not in the sense of a memorial of the dead!).

'Do this in remembrance of me.' Certainly that means re-enacting the Last Supper, but it also means re-enacting what Christ did in his death and resurrection, entering into his sacrifice, offering again the gift which he made of himself. As a very beautiful and simple canticle by D. Rimaud says:

> In memory of the saviour
> who has broken the bread for us.
> In memory of the saviour
> we shall be the broken bread
> for a new world
> for a world of love
> for the coming of days
> of justice and of peace.

It is worth noting that instead of giving us the institution of the eucharist, the Gospel of John tells us of the foot-washing: 'As I have loved you, so you are to love one another.'

That is why Christ's sacrifice is not re-enacted by a kind of magic, through formulas of consecration.

The body of Christ

Here we must recall an aspect of the real presence which remained hidden for centuries ('real' does not mean true here but under the sign of a particular reality, bread and wine).

What our faith discerns under the sign of the bread and the wine is not, of course, the physical body of Jesus of Nazareth, but the body of the Risen Lord. Nor is it only the body of the Risen Lord, and nothing but that, but also and at the same time the body he has today, the body of the Church, his social and mystical body, as theological tradition puts it. This is what St Paul meant when, reproaching the Corinthians for their selfishness at the agape, he said to them, 'Discern the body of the Lord', meaning by the body their brothers and sisters in the Church. And as we shall see in respect of the rite of communion, St Augustine went on to develop the same idea.

Given life by the Spirit

If further proof is needed, there is the symmetry of the two appeals to the Spirit (epiclesis), one over the bread and wine, the other over the assembly.

And that is logical; if the Church desires truly to celebrate the Lord's Supper, it does so to the degree that it allows itself to be penetrated by the Spirit, 'the spirit of love, the spirit of the Son himself' (eucharistic prayer for special occasions); the Spirit who speaks to us today and transforms us. And that is why there is no eucharist without the liturgy of the word.

We cannot recognize God's wonderful works without allowing ourselves to be totally involved in them, without identifying ourselves with the gift of Christ, without allowing the Spirit to make us pass over from sin to love (that is to say, bringing about a true Passover).

Looking for the coming of God

'All is accomplished' – already by Christ. But all is still in the process of being accomplished. From eucharist to eucharist, from Sunday to Sunday, we become a little more the body of Christ, both in our liturgy and in our lives which are inseparable from it (they are reciprocal, the one being a reflection and source of the other). As it becomes increasingly eucharistic, by living out and celebrating Easter under the impact of

Photo Rémy Tournus

130

the Spirit, a new world is gradually being born, a world of love, brotherhood, peace and justice, which one day will completely replace this present world. That is why our eucharists always look towards the future, are eschatological, in other words, directed towards the return of Christ.

That is the meaning of anamnesis (a word which includes *mnesis*, = memory, as in amnesia). We proclaim the death of the Lord (something which happened in the past), we celebrate his resurrection (he is living now), we await his coming again (a future event). Of these three temporal dimensions the last is the most import-

ant. It is the 'Maranatha', the 'Come Lord' which the first Christians used to cry out, words with which St Paul often ended his letters.

Remember your Church

As this Church, the body of Christ, extended through time, is slowly maturing, the progression of the eucharistic prayer leads us naturally to 'pray for' (the progression is the same in biblical prayer), 'Remember your Church'.

We pray for the Church in our age, with the Pope and his bishops at the centre, and for our brothers and sisters.

We pray for the members of the Church and all those who have lived righteous lives (unknowing members of the Church) who have already passed over the hurdle of death.

Finally, the roll-call of the whole body of Christ is not complete without including the saints, with Mary at the head, and the others whom we hope one day to join in glory.

Through him

The whole progression is summed up in the splendid and succinct formula: 'through him and with him and in him' carries the eucharist of the Church towards the Father, in the Spirit.

The eucharistic prayer is action

What I have just outlined (and whole books are devoted to the subject) is very rich. But the liturgy is not a summary of doctrinal articles. And the content which I have described, even though from time to time it ought to be the subject of catechesis (or more exactly mystical training, mystagogy), ought first of all to be lived out through symbolic actions. The liturgy is action (see chapter 4).

What does this mean in practice? We think and say that the eucharistic action is the climax of the Mass. Climax? One might prefer to say, as of Waterloo in the famous poem, 'dreary plain'! Because after a liturgy of the word which is new for every Mass, we are in familiar territory, and the congregation often switches off. For the same reason, many priests go into top gear and the congregation is left standing.

After centuries during which worshippers followed from a distance something that was going on elsewhere according to a model which worked well in theory but did nothing to further the dynamics of the eucharist (see page 128), Vatican II was anxious – and we cannot praise this too highly – to make the eucharistic prayer

intelligible. But to do this it chose a model for the eucharistic prayer in which the worshippers' participation in what was being said was limited to the Sanctus, the acclamation and the final Amen. (In this connection we might note that if the custom quickly grew up of having the whole congregation saying the 'Through him and in him', it was an instinctive attempt to overcome this frustration and not to rob the priest of his function as president, as some would have us believe.)

Without labouring the point and trying to teach the clergy their jobs, I cannot stress too much that priests should not recite but speak; that they should make the shape of the prayer felt by a pause between each section; and that those of their gestures which remain should be made with dignity, and so on.

And why is there so little variety in the choice of formularies? There are now nine prayers that can be used: I, II, III, IV; Reconciliation I and II; Children I, II, III which can be used whenever there are an appreciable number of children in the congregation. The choice of eucharistic prayer can and should be made with the day's liturgy of the word in mind (and the liturgical team will have its say, too).

Is it too much to ask priests to be creative? The first step they can take towards this is in their tone of voice; but a second is possible if, with care, they can add colour here and there to the eucharistic prayer by a short interpolation which makes the meaning come alive and recalls the liturgy of the word.

An action performed by all the people

The eucharistic prayer is an action performed by all the people (in support of this the priest never says 'I' but always 'we').

Some priests have felt that they can take the liberty of having parts of the eucharistic prayer said by the people. Although the intentions are good, this way of doing things is not to be approved of. Besides the risk here of blurring the role of the priest, a role which is essential in the Catholic faith, the texts are not suitable for being said in unison (we shall see this clearly in connection with concelebrations). Another bad solution which I am alarmed to see spreading is the practice of having the organist play during the eucharistic prayer: that only goes to prove that there is a risk of boredom.

The best step to take towards eliminating this risk is rather to allow the congregation to participate in specific areas. For example, one might imagine spoken interpolations being made at the time of the preface or the intercessions, when the general intercessions are being said. But that is above all when there is a large congregation.

As far as singing goes, the safest procedures are also the most traditional. There are some very good eucharistic hymns which can be inserted into the eucharistic action (some have been composed for this purpose). But above all, an excellent model can be found in the eucharistic prayers for congregations which include children. These have been composed (and authorized) after many years of experience of a purely verbal model and are characterized by short, sung interpolations which mark the progress of the action. There is nothing to stop this model being employed – in whole or in part – for other formulae.

Singing

We have already noted that occasional sung interventions can be made. Now for some comments on what is usually sung.

The opening dialogue. It goes back to the very first centuries, its purpose being to initiate the eucharistic action. If the priest can do so correctly, it is always a good thing to sing this.

On the other hand, singing the preface and the institution cannot be greatly recommended if the priest is not capable of intoning it. Intoning is a singing form of speech and calls for the person who does it to have the rare qualities of being both a good singer and a good speaker.

The Sanctus. The first part of the text comes from Isaiah 6 and the second part from Psalm 117 and Matthew 21.9. It is the perfect expression of the sacrifice of praise, and above all is a collective chant which belongs to the people (and not just to the choir).

The musical construction of most of the 'Holy, Holy's' which we sing is unsatisfactory in the sense that it often constitutes a prayer in itself which breaks the unity of the praise. This piece is certainly an acclamation, but at the same time it is an adoration. Few settings respect this double nature.

Concelebration

People are often moved by concelebration by a significant number of priests. Concelebrating also suits the piety towards which the vast majority of priests have been trained, making them very attached to the individual act of consecration.

But it presents two kinds of problems:
– a practical one: some sections are said by everyone, but the literary genre of the eucharistic prayer is a monologue said by the priest alone. Hence the often heavy character of these collective sayings.
– a liturgical problem. In the eucharist there is symbolically a head, Christ, represented by the presiding minister, and a body, the congregation. The symbolism is distorted when the head is larger than the body, that is to say when there is an imbalance between the presidents and the rest of the people.

The acclamation. This is equally up to the people (the priest has his own formula for the acclamation). It is addressed to Christ (the only instance in the eucharistic prayer, which itself is definitely addressed to the Father). The expression of this is on the whole enhanced by singing.

The final Amen. As I said before, the brevity of this is ludicrous when one thinks of what has just taken place. Sometimes a triple Amen is used. But there are other possibilities, for example adding an Alleluia to the Amen at Eastertide.

Assemblies without a priest

The action of giving thanks
Even though the sacrament of the eucharist cannot be celebrated because no priest is present, the whole Christian congregation is by nature eucharistic. The act of giving thanks is an essential part of this worship.

One can always do this by using the preface given in the missal. So that it can really be seen as a gesture of praise, it is a good thing to fit the proclamation in to a hymn of praise (a psalm or a canticle) or to intersperse it with acclamations (cf. the second eucharistic prayer for children).

Actions

The current eucharistic prayer has lost most of its visual impact; because it is celebrated facing the people and in the language of the people, many of the actions (or audible signals such as the bell), have become superfluous, even annoying (particularly in the epiclesis).

And yet when you think about it, everything is action.

We stand up to celebrate the paschal meal, in the attitude of those travelling in the exodus, but also of those who are risen.

'Lift up your hearts': the Eastern Churches call the eucharist anaphora (raise on high, i.e. praise, offer). The whole eucharist is a movement upwards towards God, a lifting up of our hearts (that is to say, in the culture of the Bible, a lifting up of our whole selves).

And the eucharistic action culminates, in the concluding doxology, with the lifting up of the bread and wine.

There are actions like the proclamation of the eucharistic prayer because saying is doing, and the action of singing the Sanctus (with the angels and all the saints, with the whole creation we proclaim the hymn of glory) and the acclamation (St Paul said, 'When you eat this bread and drink this wine, you proclaim the Lord's death until he comes'). No, the eucharistic prayer is not just speech nor ought it to be: one's whole being is invited to be raised with Christ towards the Father. Do we know how to pass from words to the re-creation of all these actions? The future will tell.

30

He Broke it and Gave it to Them

The communion ritual is celebrated in two parts, that of the breaking of the bread and that of communion. Originally it was celebrated with simplicity, and this still happens on Good Friday. Then various elements came to be added on which Vatican II has not pruned away. This accumulation of small rites which break up the continuity, interrupt the flow and hold up the act of communion is to be regretted. It is also important to highlight the most basic and the most traditional elements: the Lord's Prayer, the Peace, the Fraction and the Communion.

The Lord's Prayer

From earliest times it has been included because through it we ask for our 'daily bread', but also for penitential reasons: 'forgive us. . . as we forgive. . . deliver us . . .' The extension of this last request (in liturgical jargon the embolism) after the Lord's Prayer emphasizes this second intention: to approach the Lord's Table with the resolve to be converted towards God and to our fellow human beings.

The priest introduces it: the missals give three formulae, but there is nothing to prevent one from adapting the wording to match the mystery of the day. It is not a formula which one recites mechanically: 'You are to say three Our Fathers and three Aves.'

Whether the Lord's Prayer is sung (see below) or spoken, it must first and foremost be a prayer

Introduction to
The Lord's Prayer
'Deliver us' (embolism)
'For the kingdom . . .' (doxology)

Prayer for peace
'The peace of the Lord be . . .'
Sign of peace

The breaking of the bread
+ chant (Lamb of God)

Invitation to *communion* 'Happy are those'
Offering: 'This is the Lamb of God'
'Lord I am not worthy . . .'
Communion (+ chant?)

(Hymn?)
Prayer after communion

and not a recitation; or, even more, a repetition. The way in which the priest introduces it has a great effect on the collective tone and cadence. In the best cases, experience shows that the inwardness with which the congregation prays is an excellent test of its unity and the quality of its participation.

The peace of the Lord

Having been out of use for a very long time, at least among the faithful, this very beautiful rite was restored to the people of God by Vatican II. But it is sometimes not appreciated by the faithful. Two objections are often heard.

1. It is artificial to make this gesture towards someone you don't know. To this one could reply: In a moment you are going to take communion with this unknown person! Doesn't that worry you? Isn't it because offering the peace involves your body more than communion does? Offering the peace forces you to come out of yourself, out of that reserve, that inclination to keep yourself to yourself, which you tend to have above all in Church. When it comes down

to it, I am ready to believe that the way in which you feel about this gesture is a good indication of whether you are really living the liturgy with all your being.

2. Another objection is that it is not a sincere act because we are never really at peace with other people. This is a more serious objection. It implies that we should never take communion together, because we shall never live in perfect unity. We say, 'Lord, I am not worthy,' and then we go up to communion. Before making the gesture of the peace, we should say, 'Lord, my love falls short.' This objection touches on a point which is fundamental to the Christian faith: the gesture of offering the sign of peace is first and foremost an acceptance of the peace which comes from the risen Lord and therefore is a conversion, not a voluntary effort; it is also the proclamation of a peace which has already been received through Christ, but is still to be made and which will be completed and fulfilled at the end of time. This dimension of welcome and this prophetic character of the act of giving the peace is, moreover, found in all Christian celebration. It is in this sense that one ought to think of the gesture of the peace.

In practice, a great deal of freedom is allowed in how this gesture is made, and what form it takes. It is a point where one sees whether the liturgy holds together. If the congregation has not been really welded together during the course of the Mass, then it is useless and inappropriate to perform this action.

The fraction

'They recognized him in the breaking of the bread.' This is one of the terms which the New Testament uses to denote the eucharist. That indicates its importance, and it is fortunate that Vatican II has reinstated the gesture. In theory, at least, but after twenty years or so, what in fact has been done?

The reason for this inactivity is quite simple.

Photo Rémy Tournus

137

There is no fraction, i.e. no expressive act of breaking apart, because there is virtually nothing to break except a 'host' of 8cm in diameter and about the thickness of a visiting card. Here we must read what is said by GIRM:

> The nature of the sign demands that the material for the eucharistic celebration appear as actual food. The eucharistic bread, even though unleavened and traditional in form, should therefore be made in such a way that the priest can break it and distribute the parts to at least some of the faithful. When the number of communicants is large or other pastoral needs require it, small hosts may be used. The gesture of the breaking of the bread, as the eucharist was called in apostolic times, will more clearly show the eucharist as a sign of unity and charity, since the one bread is being distributed among the members of the family (GIRM 283).

That is quite clear! A 'food'? This tasteless, flavourless, thin (two-dimensional) bread which provokes the inevitable question from children, 'Mummy, what are you eating?' (and the poor mothers have to explain to them that it is bread, but at the same time that it is not bread!) How fortunate are Christians in the East who have adopted unleavened bread, and for whom the body of Christ really tastes of bread: 'I am the living bread . . . Taste and see how gracious the Lord is . . .' Realism of the sacrament . . . and real presence!

So taking into account the demands of convenience, we should at least try to observe the minimum sought by the ritual. When it is not possible to share the bread amongst everyone, at least it should be shared among a few people. Care should be taken to divide it out between the plates: this is also a gesture of sharing. When one sees the priest go to the tabernacle having made his own communion alone, one cannot help in all reverence thinking of a host who eats alone the meal he has just prepared and then says, 'Wait! I'm going to look in the pantry to see what is left over from the last meal.' Let us read the missal again: 'It is important that the hosts given to the faithful should be those consecrated in that same mass . . . The reason is that their participation in the sacrifice then and there being celebrated is more visibly manifested' (GIRM 56). Again the 'truth of the sign'.

The communion

It is advisable for the communion not to stretch out over too long a period, because then it becomes distribution in the bad sense of the term (forming queues). Now that the laity are able to help as ministers in this act there is no excuse for the communion to be too long.

The eucharist, the Lord's Supper, is a family meal. This significance is obviously not brought out so well when there is a large congregation. That is all the more reason for not prolonging the ritual and for paying attention to detail; for example when the communion drags or when the concelebrating priests draw it out or, still more, when a silence emphasizes the deadness of the time, there is no reason why the organist or the choir should wait to play or sing. 'The priest shares the bread of life with his brothers and sisters' (GIRM 60). In a small group, the sign of a unified family will be more obvious if the eucharistic bread is given to everyone, before they eat it all together at the same time, both priest and congregation.

In many places great care is taken over the movement towards the altar and it becomes a real procession, sometimes organized by members of the congregation.

In this way the act of communion has a chance of being seen as an act of the community and of being performed with the reverence desired.

Vatican II has restored the beautiful action described by Cyril of Jerusalem in the fourth century: 'When you come up, do not walk with

Photo Rémy Tournus

your hands wide open in front of you, the fingers spread apart, but with your left hand make a throne for the right one which is to receive the King. Then bend the palm of this hand into a hollow and take possession of the Body of Christ, saying "Amen".' The original words, 'The body of Christ', have also been restored. Augustine made a splendid comment on this: 'Do you want to understand what the body of Christ is? Hear the apostle say to the faithful: "You are the body of Christ and its members" (I Cor. 12.27). So if you are the body of Christ and its members it is your own symbol which lies on the table of the Lord, it is your own symbol that you receive. To what you are you respond Amen, and this response marks your membership. You hear "The body of Christ" and you say "Amen". Be a member of the body of Christ, so that your Amen may be true' (Sermon 372). We have already explored this symbol on page 130.

It can happen that it is physically very difficult for people to move about, for instance on important festivals, or that in a close and intimate group one wants to stress the aspect of sharing; one can do that by passing the plate from one to the other. But in such cases it must not be forgotten that some people may not wish to or may not be able to communicate, and others may wish to communicate in the old way or receive in the mouth. Above all it must be remembered that although it is a family meal, the eucharist is first and foremost a gift from above; and it is important for each person to pass on the plate with the customary words, 'The Body of Christ – Amen.'

Communion from the cup

Communion from the cup virtually disappeared for the faithful from the thirteenth century onwards, but was made possible again by Vatican II with great generosity because

> The sign of communion is more complete when given under both kinds, since in that form the sign of the eucharistic meal appears more clearly. The intention of Christ that the new and eternal covenant be ratified in his blood is better expressed, as is the relation of the eucharistic banquet to the heavenly banquet (GIRM 240).

And in the name of the truth of symbolism, how many times, we might add, have we heard the priest say 'Take and drink' when only he was drinking? Not to mention the fact that the widespread current practice is a source of unease to our Protestant and Orthodox fellow Christians.

The rite goes into minute detail over the various ways of communicating from the cup: drinking from a metal reed or from a small spoon (not very likely), dipping the eucharistic wafer in the wine, or drinking straight from the cup.

Subsidiary rites

The rites of the breaking of the bread and communion carry with them several small interventions: introduction to the Lord's Prayer, the embolism, the prayer for peace, the invitation, the showing of the eucharistic bread and wine, etc. If these formulae are repeated word for word, there is a risk of finding the rite encumbered with lifeless words. Would it be going against faith and morality to ask the priest to adapt these formulae slightly to the mystery of the day?

NB The missal includes several private prayers for the priest. There are already enough items without the priest adding these by saying them aloud!

A secondary rite is again provided for: that of commingling (mixing with) in which the priest puts a small particle of the consecrated bread into the cup. This gesture symbolizes the union of the body and the blood and the act of the resurrection. This is another piece of symbolism which is still obscure for the majority of Christians.

The purification of the cup and the plates can be done as soon as the communion is over, or after the Mass. The second course is the better. It is hardly pleasant to see the priest 'washing up', sometimes with scarcely disguised vigour, even if it is 'holy washing up'.

What is sung at the fraction and communion

As I have stressed, whether the Lord's Prayer is said or sung, it must be a prayer. Not to put too fine a point on it, apart from any aesthetic considerations, some types of music which are widely used today are not appropriate to the rite, because they get in the way of the Lord's Prayer by making it a vague hymn. When it comes to the choice of music the question is: does the music enhance the words, or do the words serve as a pretext for the music?

The triple invocation 'O Lamb of God', the remains of an old litany, is intended to accompany the act of the fraction: again it is important that this should be long enough. That is why one can make more than three invocations.

The biblical image of the lamb is undoubtedly

invoked here because of the breaking of bread which makes one think of the passion, but this symbolism is entirely secondary to that of sharing. The last response, 'grant us your peace', draws our thoughts backwards in a curious way to the gesture of peace already made.

Routine is a threat to what is sung but there are various ways of bringing it to life. Vary the content of the second part of the phrase (Lamb of God who . . .), add sung verses or sentences from the day's readings between the invocations, and so on. Finally, many of the chants could have a very significant place here, and one would rediscover the significance of the confractorium in use in certain Christian traditions.

As its name indicates, the processional communion chant, also an old tradition, accompanies the procession of the faithful towards the Lord's table. It can be entrusted to the choir, but if it is sung by the congregation it ought to include a short refrain (it is difficult to walk, eat, drink and sing at the same time!). In places where the faithful have the commendable custom of quiet reflection immediately after taking communion, the chant soon fades away and it

would be better to replace it with instrumental music where this is possible.

The hymn sung when the distribution is over has a totally different character. After the faithful have remained silent for a while (and not only them, but the ministers, too), the hymn gathers up all their private prayers into one unanimous voice. In contrast to the processional hymn, this ought to be a hymn for the people, preferably in strophic form and not alternated between a soloist and the congregation.

We should note that this is the last real hymn of the eucharist. The 'recessional hymn' is a survival from the time when, having sung the whole Mass in Latin, one could – at last – sing in one's own language. And when the priest says 'Go in the peace of Christ' he ought to go – and not say to the worshippers, 'We are going to sing Canticle no. 45.' If necessary, people could leave singing – I was going to say humming – a refrain taken from one of the important hymns of the service for one last time.

The communion hymn and the recessional hymn are obviously optional. The prayer after the communion which concludes the service normally follows on from the hymn.

Assemblies without a priest

Should one communicate at a Mass without a priest?
Some people think it best to abstain from taking communion
– so that we should not return to taking communion outside Mass, which was done in former times.
– to make people more aware of their lack of a priest, and arouse their hunger for the sacramental eucharist.

These issues are serious ones. But what right have we to deny those who are arguably the poorest the bread of life? Moreover the traditional practice of the Church (it is the origin of the reserved sacrament) makes communion legitimate because in this case it is not outside the liturgy (there is the preliminary celebration of the word) though it is outside the sacramental eucharist.

The rite of communion
The Lord's Prayer is traditionally included in the preparation for communion, and it would be a pity not to say it. As in the Mass, its penitential character can be developed, particularly if no moves have previously been made in this direction.

A gesture of peace is also a good thing to perform.

As for the act of communion, even in the absence of a priest, we should not take seriously the suggestion that people should go up to the altar and help themselves. The eucharist is always a gift which comes 'from above', and the act of receiving from another person is symbolic of this.

31

The Dismissal

This last rite has three parts: a final greeting, a blessing (which can be developed, see the missal) and the dismissal proper. Its brevity is significant: basically, if we have gathered together, it is not so that we can stay in a cosy little bunch, but so that we can once again scatter to fulfil our mission and carry out in our daily lives what we have just celebrated.

Most of the notices are given before the dismissal. Usually they deal with more than the week's Masses and their intentions, but they ought to deal above all with sharing in the life of the local Church: they do not belong only to the clergy. It is a good thing if the laity can give out some notices themselves, at least symbolically, where they are particularly involved. If the notices are lengthy, people should sit to listen to them. And so, to avoid annoying gymnastics, why shouldn't the congregation remain seated for the prayer which concludes the rite of communion?

The way the congregation goes out is often a test of the quality of the service. Are their faces closed or open, are they beating a hasty retreat or pausing to exchange words with other people? A pleasant courtyard, a room, even a coffee bar will make friendly relationships easier and go some way to recovering the fraternity of the ancient agapes.

Photo P. Lebon

143

By Way of Conclusion

32

The Liturgical Team at Work

The pastoral effectiveness of a celebration depends in great measure on choosing reading, prayers, and songs which correspond to the needs, spiritual preparation, and attitude of the participants.

In planning the celebration, the priest should consider the spiritual good of the assembly rather than his own desires. The choice of texts is to be made in consultation with the ministers and others who have a function in the celebration, including the faithful, for the parts which belong to them (GIRM 313).

And so the existence of liturgical teams is officially authorized.

What is a liturgical team?

It is difficult to give an exact reply to this question because situations and human resources are varied. In one place the team will bring together all those who take part in the liturgies (commentators, readers, musicians); in another it will bring together all people who are willing to do something, together with some of those who have a part to play in the services, others being involved in a different way; elsewhere the liturgy is prepared by district or by village.

The structure of the team is not so important. What is important is the spirit in which it works and the tasks that it performs.

Organizing the worship

1 **What is the 'mystery' that we are celebrating?**
What the missal suggests: the word
                         the rites

Tools
News-
papers
Missal

2. **What particular assembly is celebrating?**
Its make-up, its 'history', the means at its disposal, the time, the place, etc.

Starting from questions 1 and 2 make a connection between the assembly and the word (homiletic work) and establish an emphasis, a particular line

3. **List forms and material to be used**
Chants, actions, approaches, stressing a rite, etc., . . . visual

News-
papers
Books of
hymns and
chants

4. **Building the celebration**
Rhythm (emphases, contrasts, balances, 'recurrences')

5. **Looking over particular elements**

see news-
papers

This is a very diagrammatic outline of how preparation for an act of worship should be carried out. But it need not all be done by the same people. What I have called 'homiletic work' can be done by Christians who do not have special liturgical competence. Some teams, for example, will call a halt there, entrusting the rest to the specialist, and to have done that much is important. Others will stop after the first stage of the 'How?'

The first stage must not be skimped. If one gets help from books and magazines, it is to save time (above all for a good interpretation of the word of God) and not to make another restricting ritual out of what they suggest.

What is more, it is the first stage which illuminates the whole celebration. From the proclamation of the word a main line emerges, a dominant factor (not an intellectual theme). This dominant factor (in the sense that one would speak of a dominant red or blue in a painting) in no way wipes out the other riches of the ritual and biblical content, but the whole celebration is arranged round it.

It is more a question then of seeing how the rites are coloured by the mystery of the day, of finding out which rites can be brought out to best advantage in this perspective. In short, the liturgy is always the same and yet always new. Here are some examples.

The penitential section is not performed in the same way on the first Sunday in Lent and on Easter Day.

On the day when the liturgy concentrates on baptism, perhaps aspersion could take the place of the penitential rite.

On the Sunday when the word of God is the central theme, the book could be carried in procession.

On the Sunday when the cross of Christ is at the centre of the word, have it placed in a prominent position – with lights, flowers, etc, make the sign of the cross in a slightly different way to bring out its significance, and so on.

Here I have just provided some off-the-cuff examples of actions. I have emphasized that the liturgy is a matter of doing something. And it seems to me that it is first of all at this level of action that real liturgical work lies. What is more, it does not need intellectual competence, like leading the prayers or giving instruction, but quite simply a sense of action and symbolism . . . There is no such thing as an off-the-peg liturgy.

It is therefore not a question of starting the liturgy from scratch but of giving it every chance by making it our own and giving it a meaningful coherence. This is not as difficult as one might imagine.

Its spirit

However it is made up, the team ought to be characterized by:

1. A desire for friendly collaboration in which each person has his or her own place and can use his or her own gifts.

2. Concern to make the voice of the congregation heard, or rather all its voices, because the congregation is made up of many different elements. Either the liturgical team is representative of the congregation by its composition, or its members are at the disposal of the congregation, each one in a particular group.

Its task

1. Before the liturgy

– Long-term preparation. It is often forgotten that we have to begin by considering the conditions in which worship takes place. The physical space it occupies, the organization, the decoration, the implements (hymn books, for example) are also the concern of the liturgical team.

– Immediate preparation: is it absolutely necessary to prepare every service? That all depends on the capacities of the liturgical team and the number of members in it. Isn't it better to do a little and do it well?

Photo Rémy Tournus

146

2. The task of evaluation
– It is as important to evaluate a service afterwards as it is to prepare it. This is often forgotten. For example, should we change the way in which the opening rite takes place? Or should we perhaps ask what perception the faithful have of the eucharistic prayer?

The rules of celebration

However, those preparing the liturgy, particularly the person or persons in charge, who draw up the basic scheme, have to be familiar with certain rules which I shall describe, but which one can only get to know through experience.

1. The rule of rhythm. Rhythm gives meaning to all communication. This is borne out at the level of the spoken word.

In the liturgy, too, rhythm is vital. If the collection goes on for too long . . . if the preaching is the only interesting thing in the Mass . . . if the penitential process is too weighty . . . if, as often happens, after a good liturgy of the word there is a relaxation of tension (and attention) the universal significance of the Mass is falsified.

Rhythm is integral to life: the beating of our hearts, our breathing, day, night, winter, summer, etc.

Rhythm gives meaning to life: orientation and significance.

2. Duration and contrasts
Duration and contrast are what gives rhythm to worship.
– Duration, that is to say the psychological appreciation of time. A boring talk lasting ten minutes seems longer than an interesting talk which lasts fifteen minutes. Liturgy does not function by the clock. And in addition, in spite of the necessary precautions that have to be taken,
it ought always to be performed with a degree of flexibility. It is only on the spot that one can judge whether a silence has lasted long enough, or whether two or three verses of a particular hymn are needed. To do this you have to have a good ear.
– Contrast gives life, stimulates attention, brings out meaning: monotony is death.

3. The rule of unity
Our liturgies often appear to be very fragmented, especially when it comes to the singing. We have seen this in connection with the opening. Some people just pile the music on and you find Masses having ten or twelve different chants.

By contrast, when possible what is called recurrence should be used. Certain chants can punctuate all the parts of an opening rite, of the word or the eucharist. Others can punctuate each main rite.

The advantages are
– the liturgy becomes a unified whole
– there is economy in what is at one's disposal
– the congregation can more easily grasp the symbols.

This can be accompanied by other elements:
– an action, e.g. censing
– a phrase used as a Leitmotif
– a visual element.

The last rule is also very helpful when coping with the way in which ordinary Sundays succeed one another. A levelling of the fifty-two Sundays to the same shade of grey must be avoided.

And so a hymn or a visual symbol must be chosen which breaks up the ordinary Sundays (e.g. in Year A the Sermon on the Mount, or in Year C, the Gospels on riches and money. In the same way Advent, Lent, the Paschal Triduum, Eastertide will gain in unity through use of a recurrent theme.)

Know how to use all kinds of contrasts

– in position   Standing/seated/walking/
                 stationary, etc.

– in sounds   noise/silence
              music/sung words/spoken words
              musical/major or minor key, slow,
              fast, etc.
              one voice/several voices

– in forms   litany/strophe, etc.

– in content   familiar/unfamiliar
              new/old

The more I superimpose the contrasts, the stronger the overall contrast

E.g. the psalm followed by an alleluia:

seated	standing
slow	fast
minor	major
discrete accompaniment with shade	flamboyant accompaniment with light

As a contrast, here are some examples of levelling:
– the same person reads the first lesson, the psalm, and the second lesson
– the creed is broken up with short refrains and the same form is used for the general intercessions
– The priest says the eucharistic prayer all in the same tone and with the same rhythm.

Assemblies without a priest

Is a Mass without a priest a pseudo-Mass?
Some people hold that a Mass without a priest bears the least possible resemblance to a Mass. Granted, the worship has to be more flexible, but on the one hand, without doing great damage to the faith, one cannot upset the basic dynamics of the Christian assembly, which must always be worked out in practice, in this order: assembling, celebrating the word, praise and action. On the other hand, the faithful need identifiable landmarks in order to give themselves an identity.

But, one might go on to say, a Mass without a priest is a Mass without a eucharistic prayer, and there is a risk that people will not see the difference. This objection brings us back with a bump to the way in which the eucharistic action is usually celebrated. If its absence passes unnoticed, it is undoubtedly because it does not have the desired importance, weight and efficacy.